Unit Trusts Explained

The easy way to buy shares

Rosemary Burr

With an introduction by
Clive Fenn-Smith,
Chairman Unit Trust Association,
Chairman Barclays Unicorn Ltd

ROSTERS LTD
Sponsored by Barclays Unicorn Ltd

Published by Rosters Ltd
60 Welbeck St, London, W1

First Edition 1986

© Rosemary Burr
ISBN 0-948032-40-5

Filmset by JH Graphics Ltd, Reading
Printed and bound in Great Britain
by Cox & Wyman Ltd, Reading

Introduction

Thanks quite largely to British Telecom and the reduction in the tax burden on private investors, more and more people are starting to buy shares. It is vitally important that newcomers to the stockmarket obtain high quality investment management if their enthusiasm and interest is to flourish.

Unit trusts provide an ideal vehicle for new investors. They give even modest savers with just £20 a month to put into shares the chance to have top notch expert management of their money and the opportunity to invest in a broad range of companies. They are flexible and easy to buy. There is a huge variety of choice – quite simply something to suit everyone's needs from the general all round British fund to more specialist international trusts.

UNIT TRUSTS EXPLAINED guides the reader through the mechanics of a unit trust, helps them identify the correct type of trust for their situation and indicates how a unit trust investment fits into the overall financial planning process. It provides a useful introduction to the world of unit trusts and shows investors how they can make the most of the myriad of investment opportunities offered.

Clive FENN-SMITH
Chairman Barclays Unicorn Limited
Chairman Unit Trust Association

31st August 1986

CONTENTS

Chapter One
A Share of the Action

The share bug is alive and well, and flourishing in Britain today. More and more people have acquired a taste for buying shares, thanks largely to the phenomenal success of the British Telecom issue. But where do they go from there? Should they grapple with the complexities of making their own investment decisions or delegate the task to an expert?

Going Solo

Newcomers to the stockmarket quickly discover that the success they enjoyed with their British Telecom shares is rare. Few shares double over a period of six months. Dealing in shares is no motorway to millionaire status.
The main hurdles are:

● *Cost*
For the small investor the cost of buying shares makes it very difficult to build a broadly based portfolio. Taking into account tax and brokers' charges, it scarcely makes sense to consider share purchases of less than a thousand pounds.

● *Time*
To be successful in the stockmarket is virtually a full time job. You need to develop a feel for the pattern of trading and be able to empathise with market sentiment. The price of a particular company reflects not just hard figures such as profits, earnings and assets, but intangibles such as judgement about its management and the trading prospects for its sector as a whole. Since the institutions, that's the pension funds and insurance companies, play a dominant role in the market it is usually their view on a

company that is critical. Often it is difficult for small investors to put themselves in the shoes of institutions and assess companies on the same terms as the big boys.

● Information

There are two connected problems here. First, individual investors rarely have access to up-to-date information on the companies which they are considering as a potential investment. They have to rely on the company's report and accounts, a useful tool but by its very nature months old, as well as second-hand reports in newspapers and journals. Second, newcomers to the stockmarket may well find it difficult to analyse what data they can get their hands on. Few can tap into the array of computer software, which now has pride of place in most fund managers' offices, and which can be an invaluable source of research ideas, if not firm recommendations.

● Paperwork

Every share transaction involves at least one piece of paper – namely the contract note, which records the details of the transaction. When you buy shares, you will also receive a share certificate as proof of ownership. Details of share bargains and dividends must be recorded for tax purposes and entered on your tax return. Then, you will want to keep regular valuations of your shareholdings. The paper mountain quickly grows.

● Tax

Any profit from a share is subject to capital gains tax. Every year the government sets the amount, known as the allowance, which is the total capital gains you can make tax free. The allowance for 1986/87 is £6,300. Once you have used up your allowance, the tax starts to bite and reduce your profit. For long term investors, the potential tax bill after say a decade nursing shares in the same company is so huge that their holdings are virtually frozen. Before switching, they would need to believe that their new investment choice would outperform their existing holding by around 25%.

From January 1, 1987 the government is introducing a new tax-free plan for small shareholders. Called the Personal Equity Plan it will allow investors to put up to £2,400 into shares each year and provided the money remains invested for a full calendar year, all the proceeds will be tax-free.

The main advantages are:

● *Control*
You keep control over your own investments. All the shares are registered in your own name. The buck literally stops with you.

● *Flexibility*
As a small investor it can be easier to move in and out of some shares where the market is narrow. These are usually higher risk shares in smaller companies.

● *Fun*
Those with a gambling instinct may enjoy the thrills and spills of the market. Also, the satisfaction of beating the professionals at their own game if and when you do make a profit.

● *Tax-free on Small Sums*
The new Personal Equity Plan starting in January 1987 offers tax incentives, unequalled on other share investments, for small sums.

The Professional Choice
Unless you want to spend most of your waking hours studying the market, then apart from the occasional flutter the most practical action is to enlist the help of the professionals. It's here that unit trusts come into their own. They are a cheap, easy and relatively safe route to share ownership.

When you invest in a unit trust, your money is pooled with other investors and swells the funds available to be placed in stocks and shares. The investment decisions are taken by a full time professional fund manager on your behalf. Each unit holder owns a proportion of the fund which is directly related to the size of their original investment.

The main advantages are:-

● *Reduces the risk*

Most individuals can probably not afford to hold more than between five and twenty shares. In contrast, unit trusts with millions of pounds to invest can spread this sum around a much larger number of companies. The average number of holdings for a unit trust ranges from around forty to one hundred. This facility of being able to offer small investors a chance to participate in a widely spread portfolio is one of the most important features of a unit trust. Although it means that the top performing unit trust in any one year will usually underperform the highest flying share over the same period, it also substantially reduces the risks of you losing money in the stockmarket. There are no guarantees when you invest in shares. Prices can go down as well as up but at least with unit trusts you should miss the bottom of the trough, even if you also miss out on some of the peaks.

● *Professional management*

For small investors, which in stockmarket parlance means anyone with less than £10,000, unit trusts are one of the few ways you can obtain expert advice. Despite much talk about wider share ownership and the newly expressed desire of stockbrokers to embrace the investor in the street, it is virtually impossible to get a thorough and professional advisory service as an individual share investor unless your portfolio runs to six figures. True, you can receive a wealth of share tips and buying recommendations but little or no, after sales help or advice on when to sell.

Stockbrokers and investment management groups, with the best will in the world, cannot afford to allow their top fund managers to deal with their smaller clients. Instead they reserve the creme de la creme for the larger funds, which are potentially more profitable. As a unit trust investor saving as little as twenty pounds a month or investing a few hundred pounds in one go you can benefit from some of the leading financial brains in the city.

● *Cost*

Unit trusts are reasonably cheap method of investing in share while still enjoying professional management of your money.

When you buy an individual share there are charges involved at the time of purchase and again when you come to sell. Together these add up to 5½% of the value of a share bargain worth at least £1,000. When you buy units in a trust, there is an initial charge but no fee when you come to sell. Taking account of this initial charge plus stamp duty, you can expect to see about 5½% sliced off your original investment. These charges are included in the price of units when you buy them, rather than added to your bill as is the case with shares.

In addition to the initial charge, there is an annual charge which is deducted from the trust's income. Again, this is done automatically and unit holders do not receive bills for the fees. As the annual charge is subtracted from the trust's untaxed income rather than your taxed income, this is an efficient way of paying for financial advice.

● *Choice*

As an individual investor it is very daunting trying to keep track of the London market, let alone attempting to follow the vagaries of overseas exchanges. There's delays in receiving information from abroad, limited research material and the high dealing costs. Together these factors make investing overseas even for the most ardent DIY enthusiast fraught with hazards.

Unit trusts get round some of the difficulties involved in dealing overseas. As well as trusts which invest in UK shares, there's a wide choice of funds specialising in places as far afield as Australia, Japan, Malaysia and Singapore, as well as closer to home in Europe, Germany and the USA. There are also specialist trusts focusing on leisure, commodities, gold, high technology companies, financials and small companies. The annual charges on trusts investing overseas tends to be between 1% and 1¾%, compared to fees on UK trusts which range between ¾% and 1¼%.

● *Fair pricing*

The price of units directly reflects the value of the shares held by the trust. That means, roughly speaking, if the shares held by the unit trust rise by 20%, then the value of each unit in the trust also rises by 20%. There are strict rules laid down by the Department of Trade and Industry to ensure that units are priced fairly and that there is no favouritism shown either to existing unitholders, newcomers or those selling.

● *Easy access*

One of the tenets of unit trusts is that investors can, barring unforeseen circumstances, have instant access to their money. To this end, unit trusts are restricted in the range of investments, which can be chosen as suitable homes for unit holders money. Basically they are limited to buying shares and fixed rate stocks traded on the leading stock markets in the world. They cannot invest in property or physical commodities.

● *Simplicity*

Buying units is very easy. You can fill in an application form from a newspaper, magazine or trust pamphlet, you can ring the unit trust group itself or finally, go through a bank or authorised broker. To buy shares, unless they are being issued for the first time, you must go though an authorised broker.

● *Tax*

Unit trusts are tax efficient. The fund manager buys and sell shares on behalf of unit holders, and there's no capital gains tax on profits realised with the fund. All the trust's income, minus a deduction for the management fee, must be distributed to unit holders. Distributions are paid net of basic rate tax. Non-taxpayers can reclaim the money on their behalf, while higher rate taxpayers will have an individual bill. Profits on sales of units by investors are subject to capital gains tax, if your gains from all sources exceed your annual allowance.

● *Tax-free option*

Investors will be allowed to include a small holding of unit trusts in their tax-free Personal Equity Plans, avaliable from January 1, 1987.

Chapter Two
Putting Together the Jigsaw

Now that you are sold on the idea of unit trusts, let's take a look at the people who run them and how they operate. The star figure in the cast is the unit trust management group. The trustee plays a vital character part. Finally, the registrar has a cameo role.

Unit Trust Managers

Looking after the public's money is a highly responsible job. To become a unit trust manager you have to pass muster with the Department of Trade and Industry. Would-be managers have to fill in a multiplicity of forms. There's one for the management company itself and one for each of its directors. Most unit trust groups are part of a larger financial services company and this parent company is also closely scrutinised. Each parent company or shareholder has its own form to complete, as do each of the directors of the parent. What's more, if there are any changes in ownership of key personnel, then a whole new round of form filling starts swinging into action.

The rationale behind this extensive investigation into unit trust management companies, their directors and owners is to ensure that only 'fit and proper' people are in a position to look after the public's money. Apart from being honest and upright citizens, the applicants have to show they possess the investment expertise and administrative capability to handle the various aspects of the job. They also have to be suitably capitalised. At present the minimum entry requirement is £50,000, but this is rather academic.

At the start of 1986 there were 185 unit trust companies managing customer's money. Among their ranks are the high street banks, major insurance companies, merchant banks, stockbrokers and some specialist groups devoted to fund management. Since the 1984 Budget abolished life assurance premium relief, the insurance companies have been queuing up to gain unit trust management status.

Trustees

In contrast to the growth in unit trust managers over the past decade, the number of companies which qualify as trustees has remained almost static for as long as most people can remember. Thirteen companies have the position of trustee virtually sewn up across the industry. In the early seventies Law Debenture joined their ranks bringing the number to fourteen but it dropped out in 1985.

Who's who – the list of trustees

Alliance Assurance
Bank of Scotland
Barclays Bank Trust Co
Clydesdale Bank
Coutts and Co
General Accident Executor and Trustee Co
Kleinwort Benson
Lloyds Bank
Midland Bank Trust Co
National Westminster Bank Trust Co
Royal Bank of Scotland*
Royal Exchange Assurance
Williams & Glyn's*

The Royal Bank of Scotland is in the process of merging its trustee operations following the private Act of Parliament in 1985 to integrate Williams & Glyn's within the group.

As you can see from the list, the trustees are some of the biggest and richest financial institutions in the country. The high street banks, for example, take a large slice of this type of business. In many ways, it is more difficult to become a trustee than a manager. The trustees are in effect the unitholders' watchdog on the spot. They need proven expertise in the sometimes arcane area of trust law, a high degree of administrative efficiency and vast capital backing.

Registrar

Larger groups will perform the function of the registrar themselves but some of their smaller brethren have delegated this task to a specialist. The registrar records the names of all unit holders and dispatches the unit trust certificates. Unlike a shareholders register where the names of shareholders must be available at a reasonable cost to anyone who wants to see them, only the unit holders, managers, trustees or their representatives can check the trust's register.

Authorised Unit Trust

Before units in a trust can be sold to the public, the trust itself has to be given the Department of Trade and Industry's seal of approval. This process is known as authorisation. On average in 1985 the department authorised over a dozen new trusts each month – 154 in all. It's work load is increasing all the time as new groups launch ranges of seven or eight trusts in one go.

To gain authorisation the trust has to have been set up in the approved manner with a recognised trustee. The fund must be designed to fulfil a clearly specified investment objective. It cannot, for example, duplicate another authorised trust in the group's range. So you could not launch a smaller Moroccan high technology fund if you already ran a high technology Moroccan smaller companies trust. This rule is intended to prevent managers from being in a position to be able to discriminate unfairly between two trusts. For instance, favouring one trust with juicy private placements, their most experienced fund manager and a huge advertising budget while allowing the other to languish under the care of a less successful fund manager, unpromoted and used as a receptacle for lacklustre stocks. In practice unit trust managers show remarkable ingenuity in thinking up what are

FIGURING OUT THE UNIT TRUST INDUSTRY

	1975	1976	1977	1978	1979	1980	1981	1982	1983	1984	1985
1. No. authorised unit trusts	395	396	399	426	457	489	544	581	664	776	916
2. No. unit trust managers	109	NA	104	104	107	106	112	118	124	144	158
3. Funds under management £m	2,512	2,543	3,461	3,873	3,937	4,968	5,902	7,768	11,689	15,099	20,307
4. No. of trusts to which funds under management figures relate	353	352	393	421	459	493	529	553	630	687	806

Notes

1. No. of trusts (both sets of figures) and funds under management: as at 31 December each year.

2. No. of managers: as at 31 January of following year 1975–82; as at 31 December 1983–85.

NA: Not available.

Sources: Department of Trade and Industry (1 and 2)
Unit Trust Association (3 and 4)

16

really just new flavours of the month. This is partly because it is easier to promote a brand new fund rather than trying to market an existing one, even if the latter has a good track record. It's a case of unit holders thinking it's better to invest hopefully, than to arrive.

Investment restrictions

There are a number of restrictions imposed on unit trust managers.

● *Nature of investments*

Unit trusts are designed as a means of investing in stocks and shares. This excludes holdings in currencies, unless the money is waiting to be invested, commodities, property or farmland.

● *Liquidity*

Two cornerstones of unit trusts are that they offer investors instant access to their money and that units reflect the value of the shares held by the trust. In order to maintain these two valuable features a unit trust portfolio must consist of investments which can be easily sold and valued.

In practice this means the bulk of a unit trust portfolio must be placed in shares traded on one of the world's major stock exchanges. Trusts investing overseas are usually limited to 5% of their portfolio in unlisted stocks. Some trusts investing overseas specify that their portfolios will consist of smaller companies, these can boost their holdings of unlisted stocks up to a total of 25% by including, if appropriate, companies traded on the Tokyo-Over-the-Counter market and the French second market. Trusts investing in the UK can channel up to 25% of their cash into the London, Unlisted Securities Market, our junior stock market. In addition, a new variety of trust was introduced in 1986 which was devoted solely to the higher risk London Unlisted Securities Market. This carries additional warnings and statements about the higher risks involved in holding shares in stocks which are not quoted.

This stress on liquidity is also behind two other rules. First, a trust cannot invest more that 7½% of its total portfolio in a single

17

share and second, a trust must not hold more than 10% of a particular class of shares in a single company.

● *Currency*

Most unit trusts are denominated in sterling. However, there is nothing in the rules to prevent a trust investing overseas in having its units denominated in local currency, provided suitable provisions are made for customers who wish to deal in sterling.

Role Playing

Now that you have been introduced to the cast and some of the basic rules, it's time to see how each one plays the part allotted to them.

1. *Setting up the trust.*

   The unit trust management company will decide which trust it would like to launch, then consult its regular trustee who will draft a trust deed which sets out a framework for the new fund. The trust deed is in effect a contract between the managers and the trustees setting out the rules for operation of the unit trust scheme. Many trust deeds state that unit holders are also bound by the rules laid down, even though they may never have seen a copy of the deed. Copies of trust deeds are avaliable on request but usually there is a charge of between £1 and £5.

2. *Obtaining authōrisation.*

   The managers will fill in a form giving details about the unit trust scheme and return it to the Department of Trade and Industry. Along with the form will be forwarded a copy of the trust deed and a letter from the trustee, confirming its willingness to participate in a new scheme.

3. *Monitoring the manager.*

   It is the trustees' job to make sure the fund manager is sticking to the investment guidelines laid down in the trust and the objectives as first stated in the marketing material. The trustee handles all the money coming into and going out of the trust. All shareholdings are registered in the trustee's name, not the fund managers. The Department of Trade and Industry has ultimate responsibility. However, having defined the rules of the game, it leaves the trustee as referee holding the whistle.

Sources of information

On the trust's portfolio and pricing
First port of call should be the unit trust managers. If you think they are not sticking to their brief, contact the trustee. Then, try the Unit Trust Association. Finally, if no satisfaction is forthcoming contact the Department of Trade and Industry.

On performance
Talk to the managers. They alone are responsible for the trust's performance.

On unit trust certificates
Standard complaint here is the length of time these take to arrive. Contact the registrar in the first instance and then the trustee, who has ultimate responsibility for the registrar.

On advertisements
Start with the fund manager but move speedily on to the trustee if you are not fully satisfied. Again, the Unit Trust Association may be able to help. You can also write to the Advertising Standards Authority and the Department of Trade and Industry.

Chapter Three
Buying, Selling and Marketing

Right. We are at the starting blocks. The Department of Trade and Industry is satisfied with the credentials of the managers and it has given its blessing to the particulars of this individual unit trust. Units in the trust can now be marketed to the public. Surprisingly there are few legal requirements governing such advertisements. The only formal rules are that the advertisements must be approved by the trustee and that the yield must be quoted.

However, these two legal requirements are supplemented by a whole host of rules drawn up by the unit trust industry's trade association, the Unit Trust Association, which numbers about 95% of the managers as members. These include the key proviso that the price of units can go down as well as up, plus other crucial facts such as the trust's investment objective. All adverts have to conform to the guidelines laid down by the Advertising Standards Authority.

Buying units
You can buy units either direct from the unit trust managers themselves or through a licensed intermediary. The cash is paid to the managers, who in turn deduct their initial charge. On most trusts this fee amounts to 5% or 5¼%, but on trusts investing in gilts it may be lower. If the unit trust managers have a stock of units in the trust available at the time, then they will simply keep the cash and issue you with the appropriate number of units. Alternatively, the managers can transfer your cash to the trustee who will create a sufficient number of new units to cover your investments.

Creating and cancelling units

Unit trusts are what is called 'open-ended' investments. This means there is no fixed number of units available. Units can be created and cancelled by the unit trust managers at their discretion. Let's say a new trust is launched. The managers offer the units at a starting price of £1 each.

The public rush to buy and pour in £10 million. Forgetting about charges, the managers will have to create and issue ten million units. Then, shock, horror, six months later the market in which the trust is invested starts to drop in price and some unit holders want to sell their holdings. The managers will cancel the units held by the sellers and ask the trustee for cash to repay them. If there is sufficient spare cash in the trust then the managers may not need to actually sell shares from the portfolio to finance this repayment.

As you can see this process can quickly become quite long winded. People are always buying and selling units, even in trusts which are not being heavily promoted. The managers do have an alternative strategy which is designed to avoid the constant necessity of buying and selling parcels of shares as money flows into and out of the trust. Instead of simply acting as a messenger between the unit holders and the trustee, the fund managers may step in and deal in units themselves.

So if there is a bout of unit holders' selling the fund managers may decide that rather than cancelling the units, perhaps selling shares in the trust and seeing a sharp fall in unit prices, they would prefer to buy the units themselves. They then become investors in their own trusts. The rationale behind this move is that not only is it more efficient but it avoids sharp fluctuations in unit prices. It is only fair to add, that in the past few years such a strategy has generated a substantial proportion of many unit trust managers profit.

Pricing

The Department of Trade and Industry lays down a formula under which units are priced. The aim is to link the price of units with the value of the trust's investments. There are two critical parameters to remember:-

a) the ceiling or 'offer' value. This is the cost of going out and buying the shares in the portfolio afresh. It includes a sum for dealing costs.

b) the floor or 'bid' value. This is the cost of selling the whole portfolio and again includes dealing costs.

Managers cannot sell units to the public at more than the ceiling price or buy them back from unit holders for less than the floor price. The difference between the two prices is referred to as the 'spread'. The spread can be as high as 20% or 25% in a penny share fund where there is a thin market in the trust's underlying shareholdings. Normally the span is 13% for a trust invested in a range of quoted companies and less for a fund with a portfolio of gilts and bonds.

In reality, most fund managers squash the spread down to around 5½%. That's because as we have seen managers sometimes buy and sell units on their own behalf. Under the department's rules they have to create units at the ceiling price and cancel units at the floor price

Let's say the ceiling price is 113p a unit and the floor price is 100p. The trust is expanding and more money is being poured into the fund than is being withdrawn. The managers will probably sell units to the public at 113p and buy them back from the public at 107p. As the trust is expanding they won't insist on buying back the units from holders at 100p. Instead, they will probably buy the units from existing holders at 107p, hold on to these until new investors come along and then resell the old units for 113p. This gives the managers a profit to cover the administrative costs of both bargains.

But what happens in a shrinking fund? Here you have more money leaving a trust than coming in. The managers usually repay unit holders the smallest sum permitted, in this case 100p and try to attract new business by lowering the price at which they are prepared to sell units. If they are sitting on units they have purchased from the public at 107p, then they will try to break even by charging newcomers this rate. Otherwise they will have to cancel the units at 100p, giving the managers a loss.

Obviously the value of a trust's portfolio is changing daily and so is the price of the units. This further complicates the picture for the managers. When stockmarkets are rising it is relatively easy for them to make additional profits by dealing in units but when share prices are falling they have to be much more circumspect if they are not to throw up huge losses.

Paperwork

You can buy units either over the phone or by making a written application. If you telephone your order then you will be sold units at the price ruling when your request was made. However, if you send off for units with a cheque then you'll be charged the going rate when your application is received. So if you are in a hurry and want to reserve units at the current price, buy by phone.

You'll be sent a contract note, which details the number of units purchased, the price and the overall cost. If you have not already paid for the units then you should do so by return. About four to six weeks later you'll receive a unit trust certificate stating that you own a certain number of units in a specific trust. Keep both these pieces of paper safe as you'll need the contract when you come to work out your tax bill and the certificate when you want to sell.

When you wish to sell, you again have a choice. You can pick up the phone, making sure you have all the details about your holding to hand. Alternatively, you can sign the back of the unit trust certificate and return it to the managers. Again, much depends upon your view about prices. Obviously it's speedier to sell by phone. If you do this, confirm your instruction and the price in writing and also send the unit trust certificate duly renounced on the back to the fund managers as quickly as possible. You will receive payment within seven to ten days, subject to the vagaries of the post.

Share Exchange Schemes

If you have a portfolio of shares and wish to invest in unit trusts, you may like to consider a service offered by most groups called, 'share exchange schemes'. As the name implies these are schemes which involve swopping your shares for units. Remember that as far as the taxman is concerned this process counts as a sale for the purpose of capital gains tax just as if you had decided to sell your shares in the normal way.

Unit trust groups are pretty tough about which shares they are willing to take on board. Some groups limit it to shares they are keen to buy for their various funds, others to holdings in companies which are easy to trade on the London market. Before signing on the dotted line check the terms you are being offered and see whether there is any advantage to be had over and above a private sale through your stockbroker. If you are new to the world of shares and have some holdings in new issues, which you think it is time to sell, then this is an easy and quick way of going about it.

Some groups will offer you a better deal if they plan to take the shares into one of their fund's portfolios, whereas others quote you a price formula based on the assumption that they will be selling the holding. In order to qualify for most of these schemes your share should be valued at least at £500, although some groups will not consider share exchanges unless your portfolio is considerably larger. Nearly all groups will be quite happy if your holdings total £5,000 or more. Usually you find you save money on brokerage fees or stamp duty. Sometimes the proceeds are the same as if you did the deal yourself but you are given a bonus of 1% extra units when you reinvest.

Shop around and compare schemes by all means. Ultimately, however, the key factor is to choose a trust which will provide a profitable home for your money. A good share exchange scheme is just the cherry on the cake.

Chapter Four
Surveying the Range

There are now over eight hundred unit trusts in this country. Some are relatively small with total funds of a few hundred thousand pounds, others comfortably top the £100 million mark. The industry is growing rapidly with one hundred and nineteen new trusts launched during 1985 and the probability of over two hundred newcomers joining the throng in 1986.

Unit Trust Boom
There are three main reasons behind this boom.

Increasing number of unit trust groups
Back in 1975 there were only 109 groups plying their wares. The unit trust industry has never accounted for more than 2% of the nation's savings, as the table shows. However, since 1981 there has been a gradual increase in numbers and funds under management. The major impetus came with the 1984 Budget, which abolished life assurance premium relief and at a stroke removed the tax advantage which life assurance plans enjoyed over unit trusts. With insurance linked packages under a cloud, companies reacted by switching their attention to the nearest alternative, unit trusts. The insurance giants did not merely put their toe into the unit trust market. Spearheaded by huge salesforces, they took the plunge with gusto. It is now quite commonplace to see the latest convert to unit trusts set up a range of half a dozen trusts before making its play for custom.

Personal Savings Market Share (%)

	1966	1969	1972	1975	1978	1981	1984
Cash	3.1%	2.9%	2.7%	3.5%	3.5%	2.7%	2.1%
Banks	10.4%	10.5%	10.3%	16.0%	13.4%	14.2%	10.0%
Building societies	8.3%	10.0%	11.7%	16.1%	17.1%	17.0%	15.9%
National savings	11.5%	9.5%	8.0%	5.8%	5.4%	5.5%	4.9%
Government bonds	7.5%	5.9%	4.0%	5.9%	4.9%	4.6%	3.6%
Company securities	26.9%	29.6%	32.0%	18.0%	14.8%	12.6%	14.3%
Life/pension funds	20.8%	21.9%	23.1%	24.8%	31.3%	34.5%	39.9%
Unit trusts	0.7%	1.4%	1.8%	1.4%	1.1%	1.0%	1.5%
Other	10.7%	8.3%	6.4%	8.7%	8.0%	7.9%	7.8%
Total	£70bn	£91bn	£127bn	£140bn	£214bn	£334bn	£570bn

Source: Quilter Goodison.

Increasing specialisation

When unit trusts first hit an unsuspecting public, the choice was limited to just a handful of different types. Most groups offered an income trust, a general middle of the road fund, a capital growth and maybe an international one. Gradually, the choice became more exotic and specialised. The collapse of the London stock market in 1974 led to a shake out. Some smaller unit trust groups were taken over and unprofitable small trusts were merged.

It is easy to see parallels between the early seventies and the urge to specialise which we are now witnessing. This is particularly apparent in the move towards ever more specialist UK trusts, investing solely in one type of company or industry, be it smaller companies, high technology or leisure stocks. However, it would be too glib to simply say this is a rerun of the 1970's. The majority of the specialised trusts are now overseas ones and this reflects in part the increasing sophistication of stock markets around the world and in part the emergence of the international investor.

Increasing interest in equities

The sale of British Telecom shares to the public in the autumn of 1984 probably marked a watershed in this country. Suddenly share ownership was not a foible of the middle classes but an activity which appealed to a broad range of people. For a few short weeks British Telecom shares were the talk of the nation. As a topic of hot gossip their prominence was shortlived but the shift in attitudes has remained. A similar switch towards equities is occurring in Europe.

Sorting out the sectors

With such a huge variety of trusts avaliable, it is essential to be able to put trusts into categories so that you can compare their performance on a fair basis. You'll find most unit trusts tend to sell themselves not on their own merits as an alternative to playing the market yourself but as the top performing trust over a specific time in a particular field of investment.

Unit trusts are divided into eighteen categories, referred to as 'sectors'.

1. *UK General*

These are middle of the road trusts invested mainly in the UK, although up to 25% of the fund can be channelled into overseas holdings. The yield on the units will range between 25% more and 25% less than the FT All Share Index, the main index of UK equities. These are best for most newcomers.

2. *UK Growth*

These are growth funds where the aim is to maximise the increase in unit price. Again, up to 25% of the portfolio can be invested overseas. As growth companies tend to pay out lower dividends the overall yield on these trusts is usually more than 25% lower than the FT All Share Index.

3. *UK Equity Income*

These are trusts where the stress is on providing a high and growing income from a portfolio of mostly UK shares. The yield is estimated to be at least 25% higher than the FT All Share Index.

4. *UK Mixed Income*

These are trusts which aim to provide a high income from a mix of shares and fixed rate stocks. There is quite a lot of leeway in the amount of the portfolio which can be placed in fixed rate stocks as this varies from 15% to 85%. The overall yield from this basket of shares and stocks will be at least 25% higher than the FT All Share Index, which of course, consists solely of shares.

5. *Gilt and Fixed Interest Growth*

These trusts aim for capital growth from a portfolio of government securities and a range of fixed rate stocks. It is a relatively new category with the first participants dating back to 1981 and now losing favour.

6. *Gilt and Fixed Interest Income*

For an income from a range of fixed interest rate stocks and a sprinkling of preference shares. At least 85% of the portfolio must be placed in fixed rate stocks and the estimated yield must be equal to at least 75% of that on War Loan Stock.

7. *Investment Trust Units*
One of the smallest sectors. This consists of trusts where at least 85% of the portfolio is placed in investment trust companies.

8. *Financial and Property Shares*
Trusts which as their name suggests earmark 85% or more of investors funds for companies which specialise in property and/ or financials. This means the trust could at any one time be invested solely in property shares, completely in financials or in a mixture of the two. Financials traditionally include banks, merchant banks, insurance companies and insurance brokers.

9. *International Growth*
A trust whose aim is maximum capital appreciation from a range of international shares, but with no consistent bias towards any particular country. To qualify as international at least 25% of the trust must be invested in overseas shares.

10. *International Income*
A rather broad category which provides a catch-all for trusts investing overseas in shares, bonds and fixed rate stocks with a view to providing a regular income. Some trusts will concentrate on shares whereas others major on fixed rate stocks and bonds. In addition, some trusts are truly international, whereas others limit themselves to a specific overseas market.

11. *North American Growth*
Trusts aiming for maximum capital growth from a portfolio of US and Canadian shares. At least 85% of the fund must be invested in the North American markets.

How the sectors add up

	Number of Trusts on			
	Jan 1 1986	Jan 1 1981	Jan 1 1976	Jan 1 1971
UK General	97	70	61	45
UK Growth	120	66	50	28
UK Equity Income	104	65	49	26
Mixed Income	20	10	9	4
Gilt and Fixed Interest Growth	26	1	4	2
Gilt and Fixed Interest Income	42	23	0	0
Investment Trust Units	8	5	4	3
Financial and Property Shares	15	12	11	9
International Growth	94	49	37	18
North American Growth	98	36	17	6
Europe	45	6	4	1
Australia	17	3	3	1
Japan	53	9	5	2
Far Eastern	53	14	6	0
Commodity and Energy	35	17	11	9
International Income	26	0	0	0
Managed	3	0	0	0

Source: Unit Trust Association

12. *European Growth*
Trusts which invest in a range of European markets or a single European bourse. Again the aim is capital growth and the floor to qualify is 85% of the portfolio in Europe

13. *Australian Growth*
Another category for those seeking capital appreciation. This time 85% of the portfolio must be invested in Australian shares.

14. *Japan Growth*
Since most Japanese shares have low yields, this is effectively a category which provides a spread of Japanese equities. The minimum requirement is 85% of the portfolio in Japanese shares.

15. *Far East Growth*
An umbrella category to mop up trusts investing in the Far East for growth which do not fall into either the Japan Growth or Australia Growth sectors. So it includes trusts which specialise in Hong Kong, Malaysia and Singapore as well as more widely spread Far East funds.

16. *Commodities and Energy*
Unit trusts cannot invest directly in commodities but they can buy shares in companies trading in commodities. This category is for trusts with 85% of their portfolios in commodity and energy companies. It includes gold funds.

17. *Managed*
A new category added at the tail-end of 1985. It covers trusts which invest in at least four other trusts run by the same management groups. So far only a handful of unit trust groups have launched this type of fund but some industry watchers predict this will be the fastest growing category in the late eighties.

18. *Exempt*
Units in an exempt trust can only be bought by pension

funds, charities and other funds which are not required to pay tax. Although there is no longer any difference between the tax treatment of portfolios held by exempt trusts and others, unit trust groups still tend to limit the purchasers to the original participating institutions.

Chapter Five
Growth Getters

The main reason for investing in a unit trust is quite simple – to enjoy a better return on your money than you would have obtained by leaving it in a building society or bank. That's fine in principle but in order to make the most of your money and your investment in a unit trust it is important to realise that comparing the returns on a unit trust with a building society is similar to comparing the virtues of say meat and bread in your diet. A balanced diet contains a range of foods and a balanced portfolio should include a variety of savings products.

Weighing up the options
Let's look at what happens when you put your savings on a bank or building society. You will be paid interest minus the basic rate of tax at a stated amount. When you withdraw your cash, you will get back exactly the same sum as you deposited. So you will have earned an income from your money but it will not have grown. In fact, if retail prices have been rising across the board while your money has been sitting on deposit then your spending power may have been depleted.

Compare this to an investment in a unit trust. You invest a lump sum in a particular trust. A set amount, usually 5%, is deducted to cover the initial charge. Usually you receive an income, called a distribution, twice a year. The sum varies and will represent your share of the flow of income into the trust from dividends paid by companies whose shares it holds. The price of your units will rise, if the shares the trust holds increase in value. On the other hand, if the value of the trust's holdings fall, then your units will decline in price. So, there are risks attached to investing in a unit trust. First, the level of income is uncertain and second, you don't know whether your money will grow or shrink.

Lessons from the past

With such risks attached to unit trusts, you may wonder why they are worth considering. The reason is that over time an investment in a unit trust has done better than simply putting your money on deposit. True, there may have been short periods when this was not the case. Say when a particular market took a dive but for long term investors prepared to tuck their money away for five years or more, unit trusts offer the chance of making substantially more of your money than a deposit. The table below compares the return on £1,000 invested in a UK general fund which clocked up a middle of-the road performance with the options of putting your money on deposit. The unit trust figure takes account of the charges you would have paid but assumes any income you received was reinvested straight away. The bank, building society and National Savings figures include accumulated compound interest.

Value of £1,000 invested after:

	5 Years	10 Years	15 Years
UK General (median fund)	£2,595	£5,266	£7,705
Bank Deposit	£1,337	£1,790	£2,212
Building Society	£1,463	£2,146	£2,917
National Savings	£1,635	£2,397	£3,233

Source: Unit Trust Association. As at January 1, 1986

The figures are just as convincing if you look at what would have happened if you had £20 a month to invest. Regular savings can smooth out the bumps and humps in a market. It takes a slightly longer period of time for the benefits to show through to the same extent as on a lump sum, but, even so, the advantages can be substantial as the table shows:

£20 a month invested over:

	5 Years	10 Years	15 Years
UK Growth (median fund)	£2,040	£6,731	£14,191
Bank Deposit	£1,384	£3,312	£5,747
Building Society	£1,487	£3,823	£7,192

Source: Unit Trust Association. As at January 1, 1986

Unit trust saving schemes are very flexible. You simply decide how much you wish to save each month and which trust you'd like your money to be invested in. You can stop, and start at will. There's instant access to your money and usually the charges are no higher than on a lump sum, but do double-check this. If you stop making payments before you have saved up to the minimum sum normally required, the unit trust group reserves the right to repay you. The minimum varies from group to group, but can be as low as £120. Ask in advance.

Timing

With unit trusts, as with all investments in stocks and shares, timing is absolutely critical. Share prices leap around in a manner newcomers to the market may find hard to credit. It may take you a year to earn 10% on your building society deposit, but a share price can rise or fall by this amount in just a few hours.

Now unit trusts are not as volatile as individual shares. The price of the units is calculated by adding up the value of all its holdings. In any one day out of a portfolio of say forty stocks, only a handful may have changed dramatically in price, and some may be unaltered. Even so, prices of unit trusts tend to reflect the trading pattern of the market in which they are invested

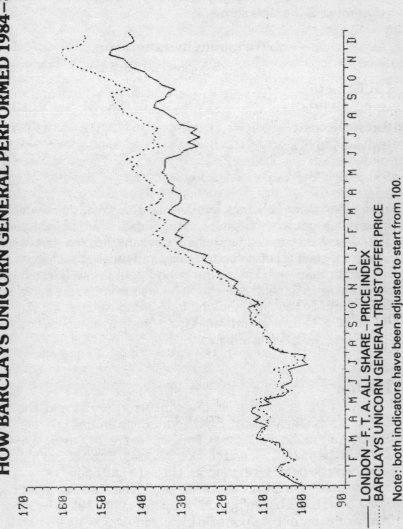

HOW BARCLAYS UNICORN GENERAL PERFORMED 1984–85

—— LONDON – F. T. A. ALL SHARE – PRICE INDEX

········· BARCLAYS UNICORN GENERAL TRUST OFFER PRICE

Note: both indicators have been adjusted to start from 100.

36

To give you some idea how important timing is let's look back to the UK market in 1984 and 1985. The graph shows you how the cost of buying units in Barclays Unicorn General trust fluctuated over the two years and puts this into perspective by tracking the prices against the FT All Share Index.

As you can see your view of the trust would have been radically altered by the date you chose to buy or sell units. As far as new investors were concerned the best time to have purchased units would have been in January 3, 1984 when they stood at 79.7p and the worst time would have been November 26, 1985 when they had risen to 128.6p. The difference amounts to 61.35%.

Now the London market is relatively mature and dominated by institutions who tend to be reasonably long term investors. It has a good spread of so-called blue chip companies, that's established businesses with sound reputations for producing solid earnings growth year after year. Such markets tend to be less volatile than smaller overseas markets often dominated by younger, less well established companies where sometimes fickle overseas investment can produce sharp changes in prices.

Specialist v General

The other important point to keep constantly in mind is the relationship between risk and reward. Put simply, the greater the risks, the higher the potential rewards or losses. If you look at the performance tables for all unit trusts you'll find each year that the winners tend to be either specialist unit trusts, say those investing in gold or smaller companies, or those investing in a particular market which has produced a marvellous performance across the board.

Turning back to 1985, the top ten was dominated by trusts which had invested in Europe. This reflected the large rises notched up by the Continental markets during the twelve month period. Other star performers were trusts which while investing in the UK had specialised in smaller companies or special situations, which had outperformed the market in general. The run-of-the mill trust investing in a broad spread of UK shares would be holding the middle ground in the performance tables.

Delving further into the past, you'll find this pattern repeating itself. Specialist funds tend to be in the winning spots year after year. The trouble is if you look down to the laggards, you'll find a greater proportion of the very same trusts dawdling at the bottom of the league as well. So the long-term record of any one specialist fund is often not outstanding.

If somebody had given you £1,000 to invest in a unit trust fifteen years ago, with the benefit of hindsight you should have placed it in a trust investing in Japan. The average fund with money in the Tokyo market would have turned your original present into the princely sum of £12,272. That's almost double the amount you would have enjoyed if the money had been earmarked for a UK growth fund.

By way of contrast, if you had been unlucky enough to decide to place your windfall in the Australian market, the end result would have been worse than stacking away the money in a building society. The average Australian trust would have multiplied your money two and half times, while it would have nearly trebled in a building society.

So for the individual investor the message is that, 'yes' there are bigger profits to be made on some specialist funds, but there are also larger potential losses. Timing can become even more crucial here. With last year's star sometimes turning into this year's recipient of the wooden spoon.

Specialist unit trusts should be used with care. They can be a useful way of building up a balanced portfolio and give you the flexibility to adjust the amount of money you invest in a particular area with greater accuracy. However, they do require much greater attention than is necessary with a general unit trust or an international fund where the decisions on which markets or sectors should be chosen is delegated to the fund manager.

Newcomers to the market may find it easier to opt for a broad-based UK trust and complement this with some exposure to overseas markets through an international trust. The results may not be so flamboyant in the short term but you shoud benefit from solid growth over a period of several years.

Managed Trusts

An alternative strategy for the novice who is attracted by the size of the gains notched up by specialist trusts but worried about making those crucial investment decisions is to choose a so-called managed trust. This is a unit trust which invests in at least four other trusts run by the same manager.

At best, it should provide small investors with the chance to capitalise on growth prospects around the world. At worst, there is no guarantee that the fund manager running the managed trust is any more certain of picking the right market at the right time than either you or an independant adviser. What's more even if the broad brush investment decisions are right, the individual trust chosen for your money may not be among the top performing in its sector.

The proof of the pudding is in the eating. Since the Department of Trade and Industry relaxed the rules to allow these types of funds to be marketed in 1985, only a handful have appeared on the scene. There are strict rules laid down to minimise the potential conflicts of interest and avoid double charging. In some cases you pay an additional fee for what is effectively an extra layer of management, in other cases it is no more costly than investing directly in the specific trust. However, there is a tax advantage. The unit trust managers can switch between trusts on your behalf behind the veil of the managed trust without throwing up a liability to capital gains tax. If you made the same switches on your own behalf in the normal way, each switch would count as a sale for the purposes of totting up your tax bill.

Chapter Six
Income Boosters

Roughly one third of the money earmarked for the unit trust is invested in funds for income. The main advantage unit trusts have over building societies as we have seen is the potential for growth. In addition, wisely picked unit trusts should provide a rising income as the dividends paid by the companies it has chosen should increase over the years. The aim of most income unit trusts is to maintain the real value of your capital by generating sufficient growth in the unit trust price to match any rise in retail prices, while at the same time paying out a steadily higher flow of distributions each year.

Type of Trusts

Unit trusts can invest in shares and fixed interest stock. Not surprisingly there are a range of trusts which by mixing these two elements can provide a variety of options for the income seeker.

1. *Maximum income now, limited growth*
   Trusts in this category are usually wholly invested in fixed rate stocks issued by governments, called gilts, or major companies, referred to as bonds. They will be found under the category 'gilt and fixed interest income'. They can sometimes pay a higher yield before tax than a building society account but don't forget there is a risk your capital may be depleted. In effect you are swopping future capital growth for extra income now. Your money is likely to be particularly vulnerable if interest rates are rising and bond prices will be falling. So you'll enjoy a higher yield but at the cost of a lower unit price.

2. *High income now, some growth*

Trusts which fall into this bracket are classified as 'mixed income'. The yield is usually considerably above that on the FT All Share Index but it is generated by a pot pourri of shares and fixed rate stocks. The proportions vary considerably, so do check carefully. As a rough rule of thumb the larger the share component the better the growth prospects but the lower the starting yield.

3. *Medium income, sound growth*

These trusts invest in shares which pay a higher income than growth stocks. On the whole income stocks tend to underperform the market, except where they become bid targets or recovery situations. The performance of individual shares can be patchy but overall the performance of unit trusts in this sector in growth terms has been excellent. If you add back into the figures a sum for net income and assume this has been reinvested and not spent, then investors in UK equity income trusts over the past fifteen years have enjoyed more growth than unit holders in UK growth funds. In fact this sector deserves a five star rating for growth along with Japan for the period from 1970–80.

Results of £1,000 invested in

	UK Equity Income	Mixed Income	Gilts and Fixed Interest Income	Japan
5 years ago	£2,808	£2,673	£1,572	£3,000
10 years ago	£5,149	£4,080	£2,983	£4,677

Source: Unit Trust Assocation as at 1st January 1986

Notes:

Assumes median fund chosen from sector. Net income reinvested and units realised at bid price.

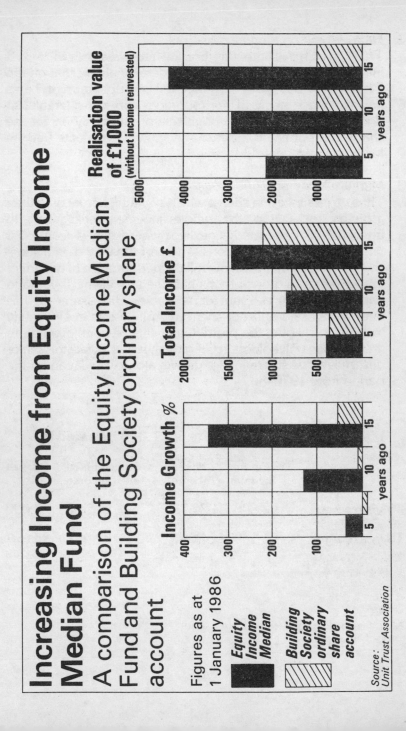

Increasing Income from Equity Income Median Fund

A comparison of the Equity Income Median Fund and Building Society ordinary share account

Figures as at
1 January 1986

Equity Income Median

Building Society ordinary share account

Income Growth %

years ago

Total Income £

years ago

Realisation value of £1,000
(without income reinvested)

years ago

Source:
Unit Trust Association

4. *International*

Most international shares have relatively low yields and fit more comfortably into growth portfolios. However, many foreign markets have flourishing dealings in convertibles. These are fixed rate stocks which pay an above average yield but give you a chance to switch into the ordinary shares of the company at a certain rate. You have a two way bet on the company in effect. You earn higher interest than on the ordinary shares but have the option to cash in on any significant rise in the share price.

Convertibles have played a major part in the portfolios of American income and international funds. They help reinstate the growth potential in a high yield portfolio. Although they are slightly more risky than ordinary fixed rate stock as part of their price reflects the market's view on the future prospects of the company's shares, they usually yield slightly less than the fixed rate stock issued by the same company. This may reduce the growth potential of the fixed rate stock if interest rates fall or the company's prospects are rerated upwards, but you are compensated by the chance to share in the higher growth prospects of the company's shares.

The most recent additions to this sector reflecting the new surge of enthusiasm for the Continent are European income funds. Some of these concentrate on ordinary shares as there are high yields to be found on Italian, Spanish and some other European stocks. Others rely on a mix of shares and fixed rate stock to produce the required level of income.

Monthly income plans

For people living off their investments the most convenient plan is one which pays a monthly income. Most groups have put together a package of their various types of income trusts to form a plan with distributions each month. The drawback is that the monthly payments fluctuate and you may end up with either a higher level of income than you need or insufficient flow of funds.

There's nothing to stop you checking the distribution dates of your favourite trusts and putting together your own portfolio. Most reputable advisers will do this for you if you ask. Alternatively some groups have devised schemes which generate a fixed monthly flow of income by linking up with a building society account. Again, you may be limiting your future growth prospects unneccesarily. A handful of groups run trusts which pay out monthly but these have not really captured the public's imagination.

Withdrawal plans

These are usually marketed as a tax free way to obtain a monthly 'income' from unit trusts. In fact, they are a mechanism for selling off a fixed amount of your capital every month or quarter and repaying it to you. The theory is that the fund will grow quickly enough to make up for the money you withdraw thus keeping your capital intact. On the tax question, the sale of the units will count as a disposal for capital gains tax purposes so you should check to see you don't go over your allowance.

On the whole these plans are not to be recommended. Frequently they promise more than they can deliver. Unit prices tend to rise and fall. The downward spiralling effect if prices start to slip will swiftly magnify losses and decimate your capital. Far better, to split your money into a sum at the building society or in national savings earning the top rate for your tax bracket and a reliable income trust investing in shares.

Yields

The return on your unit trust investment consists of two parts: an income and hopefully, capital growth as the unit price rises. The yield indicates the income you can expect to receive.

A word about the quoted yields you will see on unit trusts. The same principle applies across the board for growth and income trusts but is particularly relevant for people hoping to live off their unit trust distributions.

The advertised yield will be gross, that's before tax. It will be calculated on the basis of the historic yield on the shares in the portfolio as a percentage of the offer price, the price the units cost you to buy. So the quoted yield is based on last year dividends. It is not a hard and fast promise equivalent in status to the interest you will be paid on a deposit.

Unit trusts pay their distributions net of tax calculated at the standard rate just like the dividends on shares. Keep the distribution for tax purposes. If you don't pay tax, UK residents will be able to obtain a refund. If you are subject to higher rate tax, then you'll have an additional tax bill.

Timing

As with all investments timing your sale and purchase is crucial. With income trusts it pays to take a bit of extra care. Do not just look at the overall market trend, but examine the distribution dates of the trust. As the trust nears its payout day the unit price will be swollen with income. After it goes 'XD' the price will drop to reflect the distribution and then gradually build up again as it nears another distribution date. There is usually a time lag of several weeks between a trust going ex-distribution and you receiving your payment. The trustee will supervise all distributions and ensure you receive your fair share.

Growth point

It may seem strange but at certain times income trusts investing solely in shares may perform more strongly than growth trusts. When a market is nearing its peak, many growth stocks may be trading at very fancy ratings and looking rather expensive. Bargain hunters will focus their attention on less popular stocks and recovery situations which often tend to have an income tag. That's basically because up till now they have needed a large yield to attract investors to support what may be lacklustre management or an ailing industry. Many income stocks have valuable assets such as freehold property or could be revitalised with new management, so at this stage in the market's lifecycle they attract the attention of unwanted bidders. This usually leads to sharp rise in their share prices and handy profits for investors.

Income stocks, and by extension income trusts, can also come into their own when a market is slipping lower. The higher they fly, the faster they fall – adequately sums up many growth stocks. Income stocks by contrast often trade within a much narrower range. They may not rise as quickly as growth stocks but they won't leave such a big hole in your pocket if things turn sour. So for the cautious, beginners or those who feel the market looks a bit expensive income trusts can be a useful vehicle.

Charges

The annual charges on UK income trusts tend to be the lowest in the industry. It's not that it is any cheaper to run an income fund but as the fee is deducted from the trusts income, fund managers keep it low so as to boost the fund's yield. Typical annual charges range from ½% to ¾%, the latter figure being the norm.

Name of the game

Don't be confused by names such as 'higher income' or 'extra income'. There is no fixed scale which justifies these labels. Indeed a group's higher income fund may yield less than it's income fund. The crucial point to discover is whether you are looking at a trust which invests solely in shares, i.e. equity income category, or one which adds fixed rate stock to its portfolio, the mixed income category, or even one which falls into the general category of maximising overall return.

Example of how the classfication works:

Assume the FT All Share Index was yielding 4% gross.

UK General – 75% in UK shares plus yield of between 5% gross and 3% gross.

UK Equity Income – at least 85% in shares and convertibles. At least 75% in UK shares. Yield of 5% gross.

UK Mixed Income – Yield of at least 5% gross with between 15% and 85% in fixed interest securities.

So far all the international income funds have been bundled together. Don't be too impressed by talk of a trust being among the top performing in this category. It's such a mixed bunch, comparisons are pretty meaningless.

Chapter Seven
Foreign Forays

Sixteen years ago there were less than thirty unit trusts which invested overseas. They accounted for 18% of the total number of trusts. Today, international trusts dominate the performance tables, the list of new launches and are among the most successful long term investments across the range of unit trusts.

	UK	**International**
1985	467	389
1980	269	119
1975	199	72
1970	126	28

The cult of the internationally invested unit trusts holds considerable sway at present. The terrific rises notched up by Japanese invested trusts in the early eighties coincided with a revival in the fortunes of the unit trust industry. Many a newcomer was weaned onto the idea of unit trusts after reading about how investors had doubled their money in twelve months by investing in Tokyo. In fact, Japan aside over the past fifteen years long term investors would have fared better by staying at home as the table, Around the World shows.

International choice
The sheer range of unit trusts channelling money overseas is dazzling. Most major markets have trusts specifically devoted to them and brave souls willing to bet part of their shirt on the Thais or the Phillippines can find something to cater for their tastes in the

Far East category. Then, there are the latest breed of international income funds, which rely on a mix of shares, fixed rate stocks and those half way houses, convertibles, to generate a higher level of income than usually enjoyed overseas.

The bulk of overseas trusts are unashamedly aimed at maximising growth. The overall yield on many of these markets, particularly in the Far East, is negligible and it is usually only by going for fixed rate stocks or those hybrid convertibles that a decent income can be maintained.

Industrial spread

One of the advantages of international trusts is that they allow UK investors to invest in some of the world's greatest companies from the comfort of their sitting rooms. You can choose from the Australian market, dominated by natural resource stocks, through to Tokyo, with its consumer and electronic companies, around the globe to Frankfurt, with its solid financial institutions, engineering and car manufacturers. Give the world a further spin and you have the property and textiles giants in Hong Kong, the plantations and commodities of Malaysia, the retailers, computer and electronic specialists in the US. All these complement the range of companies you can invest in here at home.

Spreading your money across the world and through various sectors may reduce the risks. Imagine all your money was concentrated in say UK retailers. Interest rates rose, money flooded into the pound, putting up its value and a flood of cheap Japanese consumer goods cornered the market. British retailers suffered from a profits squeeze while returns on Japanese exporters soared. There's always a winner and loser in every transaction – and British companies are not always on the winning side.

Currency risk

As well as the benefits you may obtain in terms of reducing your risk by spreading your money around the world's stockmarkets, you are also throwing up a whole new layer of potential profits or loss. That's currency. With an international trust you have two sources of growth – the share holdings and the currency. To see how this works, look at the following examples:

a) The share price rises and sterling strengthens against the dollar. You invest £1,000 in American shares when the pound stands at $1.20. This gives you a portfolio worth $1,200. Six months later the price of your shares has risen by 10% valuing your holding at $1,320. Sterling has strengthened against the dollar and now stands at $1.50. You sell your shares and convert the proceeds into sterling. You receive £880 – that's a 12% loss!

b) The share price rises and sterling weakens against the dollar. You invest £1,000 in American shares when the pound stands at $1.20. This gives you a portfolio worth $1,200. Six months later the price of your shares has risen by 10% valuing your holding at $1,320. Sterling has weakened against the dollar and now stands at $1. You sell your shares and convert the proceeds into sterling. You pocket £1,320 – that's a 32% profit.

c) The share price falls and sterling strengthens against the dollar. You invest £1,000 in American shares when the pound stands at $1.20. This gives you a portfolio worth $1,200. Six months later the price of your shares has fallen by 10% valuing your holding at $1,080. Sterling has strengthened against the dollar and now stands at $1.50. You sell your shares and convert the proceeds into sterling. You end up with £720 – that's a 28% loss.

d) The share price falls and sterling weakens against the dollar. You invest £1,000 in American shares when the pound stands at $1.20. This gives you a portfolio worth $1,200. Six months later the price of your shares has fallen by 10% valuing your holdings at $1,080. Sterling has weakened against the dollar and now stands at $1. You sell your shares and convert the proceeds into sterling. You net £1.080 – that's an 8% profit.

50

The table shows how share prices have moved over the last ten years in 11 major financial markets. Column A shows the average annual return in local currency and Column B translates these gains into sterling. Over the 10 year period 1975 – 84 sterling's weakness against the major world currencies helped boost the return for UK investors overseas.

So the message is, if sterling is stregthening against, say, the dollar, then you will need less and less pounds to buy each dollar and conversely your dollar holdings will be worth less in sterling. If sterling is weakening against the dollar, you will need more and more pounds to buy each dollar but your holdings will be worth an increasing number of pounds. In an ideal world you would buy units when sterling was at its strongest and sell when the pound was at its weakest.

How Currency effects the Return on International Equities

% per annum	COLUMN A Annual returns in local currencies Average 1975–84	COLUMN B Annual returns in sterling 1975–84*
USA	14.8	23
Japan	14.8	25
United Kingdom	31.7	32
Canada	15.4	20
Germany	12.5	16**
Australia	18.1	21
Switzerland	10.0	18
France	19.4	19
Singapore	17.9	27
Netherlands	22.2	27
Hong Kong	26.6	30

* Figures have been rounded up
** Excluding German tax credit   Source: Phillips & Drew

Hedging

There is a way unit trusts can rid themselves of this currency risk at a stroke. It's called hedging. It means protecting the trust against any subsequent change in the exchange rate of sterling against the currency in which the shares are dominated. There are various methods of doing this which involve options, futures and back-to-back loans. Under the current rules unit trust managers are restricted to this latter route, the back-to-back loan. This can be cumbersome and depending upon the difference between interest rates on sterling and the chosen foreign currency, may work out quite expensive.

For investors in overseas trusts the main problem is relying on the managers being astute enough to pick the right shares and second guess the international currency traders correctly. This is a tough task and one many management groups have not proved too clever at handling. The poor performance of both US and Japanese trusts in 1985 was partly due to wrong footing on the currency front, particularly in the case of the dollar.

Many fund managers appear to have learnt a salutary lesson from their experience during 1984 and 1985 with the dollar. If timing is critical in shares, it is the be-all and end-of-all in currencies. It's no good thinking the dollar is going to fall in the summer of 1984 and then hedging the trust, if it continues to rise until Spring 1985. You will have lost out on currency profits in the intervening period and had to finance the hedging operation.

Most groups are now more willing to let the trust remain unhedged, except in very extreme circumstances. After all, they argue with some justification, if investors wish to have money in Wall Street or Tokyo it's because they believe the overall profit potential of both the shares and currency is attractive.

Market constraints

Just because it's simple to invest in a trust with a UK portfolio as one with say an Australian list of shareholdings, don't be fooled into thinking your money is equally safe. Ask any fund manager about the difficulties involved in investing in certain overseas markets and you'll be regaled with tales of woe from now to next lunchtime.

London is a well regulated market. It is relatively easy to deal in quite large parcels of shares in most major companies. Information about quoted companies flows reasonably freely among the investment community and the rules are designed to ensure that all shareholders stand as one among equals when it comes to bids and deals. The same cannot be said for all the stock markets around the world. In addition to the varying levels of supervision and discrepancies in ethical standards, there are problems of various time zones and language barriers. The result is all too often a recipe for confusion, frustration and poor investment performance.

The larger international markets are not so prone to these complaints. Some fund managers even argue that distance creates clarity. They say overseas investment managers can do better at stock picking than their local counterparts. This may be true but when it comes to getting the choice of new issues, private placings and stock in smaller growth companies, foreigners may find they are at the bottom of a very long queue. Improvements in international communications are breaking down some of the barriers, but formidable cultural walls remain to be breached.

Political risk

In some countries, including Australia, overseas investors are treated almost as second class citizens. They are limited in the amount they may own of a company and this can lead to them being excluded say when a rights issue is made. Under a rights issue existing shareholders have the right to buy a certain number of new shares, the exact sum being calculated in direct proportion to their existing holding.

Elsewhere you may run the risk of the government deciding to ban all foreign shareholders in local companies. Overnight holdings can be repurchased or seized. Finally, there is the ultimate problem of civil war erupting and closing down the market entirely.

Unit trust investors are usually better placed than individual shareholders. Only the major developed markets currently sport unit trusts devoted solely to a single exchange. In recent years the trend towards trusts investing in more speculative markets has

AROUND THE WORLD

£1,000 INVESTED IN:

	UK Growth	International	North America	Europe	Australia	Japan	Far East
5 Years Ago	£2,340	£2,160	£2,099	£3,192	£681	£3,000	£1,675
10 Years Ago	£5,120	£4,069	£3,392	£5,512	£1,715	£4,677	£4,168
15 Years Ago	£6,800	£5,805	£4,637	£5,871	£2,547	£12,272	*

£20 PER MONTH INVESTED IN:

	UK Growth	International	North America	Europe	Australia	Japan	Far East
5 Years Ago	£1,942	£1,759	£1,712	£2,564	£1,029	£2,160	£1,607
10 Years Ago	£6,362	£5,557	£5,543	£9,203	£3,002	£6,624	£5,393
15 Years Ago	£12,725	£11,000	£10,211	£11,505	£5,573	£13,190	*

Source: Unit Trust Association

Notes: As at 1st January 1986

Assumes money was withdrawn from unit trust at prevailing bid price.
Net income reinvested over the period.
The performance reflects the median fund in the sector.

* No trust in existence then.

started to grow. Singapore, Malaysia, Frankfurt and Hong Kong would find it difficult to support the current level of trading if the foreigners cashed in their chips, yet UK investors can, if they choose, place all their money in trusts specialising in each of these markets.

Charges

Generally the charges on overseas trusts are slightly higher than on UK funds. This reflects the greater expenses involved in buying shares overseas and researching foreign companies. Whereas most UK trusts charge an annual fee of ¾% to 1¼% on overseas trust this is likely to be in the region of 1% to 1¾%. The initial charge is normally the same at a standard 5%.

Security

The risks of your money going astray while invested in an overseas unit trust should not be any greater than those involved in trusts with UK portfolios. The trustee plays the same role as usual and all holdings are registered in its name. An overseas trustee of equal standing may be used to simplify matters and avoid the necessity for share certificates to be whizzing around the world. However, if the overseas trustees failed to do its duty, the UK trustee would have to reimburse unit holders and in turn seek to recover the money from the overseas trustee.

Chapter Eight
Offshore Options

Offshore funds are not authorised by the UK authorities but are subject to local regulations. They can be based as near as 100 miles in Jersey or as far as 3,445 miles away in Bermuda. In many respects they are run in a similar way to unit trusts here at home. However, as they are unauthorised by the Department of Trade and Industry they may not be freely marketed in this country.

If you can check that the fund is linked in some way to a reputable unit trust management group or well known British bank, then you should be on safe ground. Unfortunately, the quality of regulation in some offshore centres leaves something to be desired and it is best to steer clear of unfamiliar managers whose funds are based on some islands you need a map and a magnifying glass to detect.

Safety
Just as the quality of the fund managers may vary, so the safety aspects need to be examined with care. You'll find either a trustee or custodian installed to protect unit holders' interest. Make sure this is an institution of repute, one of the world's major banks for example. Avoid trusts where the custodian has less clout than the fund manager or is not backed with sufficient capital to bail out unit holders in the event of any problems.

The standards imposed by regulatory authorities vary a great deal. In order to attract funds to these tax havens, they have to be seen to be providing a minimum level of protection. Otherwise a series of scandals will leave a sour taste in investors mouths and lead fund managers to swop location. Stick to centres in your own time zone such as Jersey, Guernsey and the Isle of Man.

Tax

Gains within the trust are allowed to grow tax free. The trust receives dividends from the companies in which it has invested. These dividends may be taxed by the countries in which the companies are based. When the dividends are distributed to unit holders, they are told how much tax has been paid already and must then settle their own tax bill. Under laws designed to prevent income being rolled up into capital gains which were then taxed at a lower rate, offshore funds have to distribute 85% of their income. Currency funds have in addition to distribute a similar amount of their gains on currency swops. If this is not done, any gains you make by selling your units will be taxed as income. That aside, for UK residents profits to units are taxed in the same way as if you had been investing in an authorised unit trust. However, there is one loophole from which you can benefit. Umbrella finds are offshore companies which have several classes of shares. Each class represents an investment in one of the sub-funds. You can swop between sub-funds without making a sale for tax purposes.

Pricing

There are no fixed rules. Some trusts are priced at net asset value, others operate in a similar way to a traditional unit trust with a 5½% spread between the buying and selling price. Do read the small print carefully.

Charges

The rules governing UK authorised unit trusts are very strict about what can be charged against the fund. The starting up costs and the trustee's fee, for example, come out of the manager's pocket. No such regulations exist overseas. You'll need to scrutinise the small print.

The initial and annual charges may be higher overseas. The average initial charge in this country is 5% but offshore funds tend to be more in line with the US, where 7½% is fairly standard. Annual charges also vary. In the UK the annual charge is deducted from the fund's income but overseas some income orientated trusts take the fee from the trust's capital. Check the prospectus.

Buying and selling

Units are bought and sold by the managers. Often dealings are restricted to one day a week or even monthly. Check this in advance. The fund managers may in certain circumstances exercise the right to suspend repayment for up to six months. Check the prospectus. Information on offshore funds can be obtained from your bank, stockbroker or professional adviser. Unlike authorised unit trusts these cannot be advertised in this country. Some groups have circumvented this restriction by obtaining a stock market quote for their shares so they can put a prospectus in the newspapers, and you may see offshore funds which are quoted on the London Stock Exchange advertised.

The Advantages

There are three main reasons for using offshore funds:

a. you can't find a suitable unit trust in this country. For example, you want to invest in currencies

b. you want to actively switch between various trusts within one group without throwing up a liability to capital gains tax. Then choose an umbrella fund

c. you want your money offshore, either because you plan to live and work overseas or because you want to be free to move it around the world and fear exchange controls may be reintroduced preventing you taking large sums out of the country.

Expatriates

Most UK unit trusts are denominated in sterling. Although the Department of Trade and Industry has no axe to grind against trusts being denominated in the currency of the locality where the money is invested, few have taken up this option.

Those living overseas are often paid in dollars or the local currency. Offshore funds provide them with the flexibility to invest in non-sterling pooled investments. They are a more tax efficient method of investing in markets outside the UK for non-UK residents. Some offshore funds roll up their income into the trust and this helps boost overall growth at a time when you may not need income. To gain maximum benefit of this facility the units should be sold while you are non-residents for tax purposes.

Flexibility

The offshore funds can be used either as a channel for regular savings or as a home for lump sums. Many expatriates find they can afford to save large sums of money on a regular basis and a monthly savings scheme which unlike a life assurance plan can be stopped or started at will is very useful. Alternatively, those who expect to be dividing their working lives between periods abroad and spells back home may prefer to consider the option of taking the life assurance route. Provided the plan is cashed in while you are overseas this allows your money to build up tax free within the fund without distributing any income over a ten year period, even if part of that time is spent working in the UK.

Warning Note

Do stick to offshore funds run by managers whose name is well known in this country. If possible try to choose those which are run from offshore islands such as Guernsey, Jersey and the Isle of Man where they speak English. If anything does go wrong it is easier to track down the problem in Jersey than in the Seychelles.

Performance

It is difficult to compare the performance of offshore funds with unit trusts. Many offshore funds are denominated in dollars and the managers' aim is to maximise returns in that currency. On conversion to sterling, the performance may be either marred or improved depending upon how the exchange rate between the pound and the dollar has altered over the relevant period.

Chapter Nine
Portfolio Planning

You don't have to be a financial whizzkid to make the most of your money. The key to success is long term thorough planning to make sure you, and your family's needs, are covered in the most flexible and tax efficient manner.

To give you some idea of the part unit trusts can play, let's take a look at some situations which crop up regularly. The examples below are illustrations. Readers should seek individual help from professional qualified advisers who can tailor their recommendations to suit the current tax, stock market and investment conditions.

Kid's Stuff

Ten year old Harry inherits a £5,000 legacy. His parents wish to use the money to build up a cash sum for when Harry leaves school. What should they do with the money?

Under normal circumstances the Inland Revenue assumes that money in the child's hand is part of the parents' income. However, in the case of a legacy the taxman agrees that this money is in fact the child's and the income on it does not need to be added to the parent's income. So, assuming Harry has no other income, part of the legacy could be put on deposit to generate some tax free pocket money. As Harry does not pay tax, the best place to deposit the money would be the National Savings Bank investment account, which pays interest gross, ie with no tax deducted, or an offshore bank account.

For the bulk of the legacy Harry's parents will be looking for an investment which is both flexible – they don't know when Harry will want to draw out the money – and will provide long term growth, preferably to outmatch inflation. The growth element will need to come from some type of investment in shares, either direct or through a package, such as a unit trust. Given the size of the total to be invested unless Harry's parents are share experts, a unit trust is the best option. The unit trust should be put into the parent's name designated with the child's initials. This avoids the money being frozen until Harry is eighteen and deemed to be capable of making his own investment decisions. Harry's parents could divide the money between UK general, UK growth and an international trust. They can reclaim the tax paid on any distributions of income from Harry's unit holdings, provided these do not exceed his personal allowances.

William's parents would like to set aside a small sum each month for him. At present they can afford to save £50 every month. What should they do?

As far as the taxman is concerned this monthly sum will be treated as if it were regular savings made by and for William's parents. So the tax treatment of the investment becomes crucial. Tax free National Savings Certificates, sold in denominations of £25, are ideal and available from the post office. If the money is put on deposit then any interest will be taxed at William's parents highest rate, so that's not a sound option. Similarly, income from a regular unit trust savings plan will be taxed at William's parents rate while he is their responsibility and when sold any gains will be added to the couples for the purposes of calculation of their capital gains tax bill.

If William's grandparents wish to give him a small but regular sum, then an extremely tax efficient method is to set up a covenant. Under this his grandparents agree to pay William a certain sum for a period of at least seven years. Every £710 given in this way is boosted to £1,000 by the taxman. William's parents can recover the additional sum from the taxman for their son. This is an effective way of using up William's tax allowance and only works when he does not have earned or unearned income from another source, such as a legacy, where his personal allowance is exceeded.

Starting Out

Margaret is eighteen, lives at home and has just started to work at a computer company nearby. She has no other income but her parents won't accept money from her as a contribution to the household expenses. How can she best save up enough money to leave home.?

To start with Margaret should tackle the basic skills of money management. Opening a bank or building society account and learning how to make her salary last the whole month. After a few months she can start working out how much money she can afford to save on a regular basis. Then she should try to put some money into a building society or bank account every month to build up a lump sum for holidays, car or perhaps, eventually a mortgage.

Margaret's grandmother gives her £2,000 as a 21st birthday present. What is the best place to invest this sum?

The first thing to do is pay off any debts – credit card balances which have been left to grow, overdrafts or loans on, say a car. The balance should be used as part of the deposit on Margaret's first home or to cover the expenses of moving and furnishing.

Family Fare

Andrew and Elaine are both twenty-five and have been married for one year. They have no children. There's not much spare cash to be invested after they have made their mortgage payment. They want to put their finances on a sound footing, what should their priorities be?

First insurance. If their mortgage is from a building society or high street bank, it's probable that they have been advised to take out cover for their belongings and the home itself. If not, they should do this straight away and make sure that the sum covered is sufficient by reviewing their policy every year. Then, they should buy some cheap life assurance. The best bet is what is called 'joint life cover' and it should include some family income protection if they are planning to have children in the near future. This means that if anything happens to either Andrew or Elaine, the remaining partner will have a financial cushion. They should also check or make their wills.

If there's any spare cash left over, a certain sum should be set aside for emergencies, such as car repairs. This can be placed in a high interest bank account or building society gold account. Additional cash not likely to be needed in the near future can be invested for long term growth in the most tax efficient manner. Generous tax relief is available on pensions, both Andrew and Elaine should take full advantage of this, if possible.

Five years later, Andrew's father dies and he receives a £20,000 lump sum. Andrew and Elaine now have two children. Elaine works part-time. How should they use the money?

First, don't rush to pay off the mortgage. Home loans up to £30,000 are very tax efficient at the moment and with house prices rising there should be a tidy profit. Second, much depends upon whether the couple need the extra income straight away or whether they can afford to invest the money for the longer term. In both instances it is important to try to protect the real value of the inheritance by investing some part of it in shares, either direct or through a growth or income unit trust.

If the money is going to be earmarked for the children's education then a mix of life policies, gilts and shares or unit trusts would be appropriate. If the family would like a little extra income, then a mix of National Savings gilts and unit trusts would fit the bill. Andrew and Elaine should sit down and go through their finances. Once they have decided what they would like to achieve with their money, they should seek professional advice.

Middle Aged Spread

Edward and Linda are self-employed. Together they run a fast food franchise. They don't have much time left over for managing their own financial affairs. What should they be doing?

Man's best friend may be his dog, but a self-employed person's most effective adviser is usually an accountant. An accountant will be able to tell Edward and Linda the best way to maximise their spare cash, particularly how to take full advantage of the flexibility built into many of today's tax efficient personal pension plans. They should also be able to give helpful hints on how best to obtain adequate life assurance cover and reduce any future inheritance tax bills.

If there's any spare cash to be invested after these matters have been considered then much depends upon the couple's time-span. A ten year maximum investment plan could have tax advantages if Edward and Linda were certain they would not need access to the capital over the next decade. Probably a better bet would be to consider a mixture of gilts, shares and unit trusts, depending, of course, on the size of the sum to be invested and the rest of the couple's finances. For out-and-out growth a mix of UK growth funds and international trusts may be most suitable.

Approaching Retirement

In the run-up to retirement most people will be trying to build up a lump sum they can live off once their monthly pay cheque stops. So, what are the best tactics of maximising today's earnings to provide for the future?

First, review your current commitments. Many people find they are living in accommodation which is now too large. Their children may have upped and left them rattling around in a house with several empty rooms. Moving to smaller accommodation can generate some money for investment. Those in employment should take full advantage of any opportunities to invest further in their pension. High rate taxpayers may wish to consider some form of ten year savings plan such as a regular premium qualifying whole of life assurance policy and also some form of equity investment, either direct or through unit trusts. Depending on the amount of money to be invested and the complexity of your tax affairs, you may need to consult an accountant and/or a professional adviser.

Home, Sweet, Home

Phillip and Fiona retired last year. Their savings were geared towards growth and now they need to boost their income, while hopefully maintaining the value of their capital. They also took a lump sum payment from their pension entitlement. What should they do?

They need to work out exactly how much income they would like to see whether it is feasible to generate this sum, while still investing their capital for some growth. Investment decisions should be taken only after the tax implications have been examined in full. Much will depend upon the ages, health of the couple and whether they wish to leave money to friends, relatives or children. Most people will need a mix of cash, deposits such as National Savings income bonds and insurance company fixed rate bonds, gilts and some equities. Income unit trusts can be very helpful here as they provide the chance of a growing income plus the potential of guarding the real value of the couple's savings. If money is very tight, the couple may need to consider an annuity or releasing some of the equity in their house.

Financial Planning

Planning your finances requires time, effort and skill. Never be afraid to seek professional help. Stick to your bank, stockbroker or a member of the Financial Intermediaries, Managers, Brokers Regulatory Association – FIMBRA for short.

In order to make the most of the financial advice available you should be clear in your mind what you require before seek ing help. This will make the adviser's job easier and also remove the nagging worry many people have that they will be talked into unwanted investments.

HAVE YOU MADE 710% OVER THE LAST 10 YEARS?

If you'd invested £1,000 in our General Trust over the 10 years from 2nd June 1976, your holding would be now worth £8,100, on an offer-to-bid basis with net income reinvested. Read on and fill in the coupon on page iv for more information.

STOCKS AND SHARES FOR BEGINNERS. START WITH £20.

Our Monthly Savings Plan lets you invest in the stock market without having a lump sum to start with.

If you can save a regular amount, even as little as £20 a month, we will invest it in stocks and shares via units in our highly successful General Trust.

Well-run unit trusts such as our General Trust offer better long-term potential for capital and income growth than a building society or National Savings.

But remember that unit values can go down as well as up.

Your monthly sum will be managed by the team of Barclays Group experts who already look after more than £1,300 million for our unitholders.

Send us the coupon overleaf and we'll send you the details.

WHAT'S THE BEST THING TO DO WITH £20,000?

Whether a sudden windfall or the result of years of saving, a large sum of money always raises two important questions.

Where's the best place to put it? And where to go for informed advice?

Barclays have a team of highly skilled professional advisors, who specialise in the investment of larger sums.

They're called District Services Managers and

they're ready to help and advise you, free of charge, whether you bank with us or not.

They recommend a spread of investments, including some with Barclays, if appropriate.

But all will be tailored to your personal financial needs, be they for income, capital growth or a combination of both.

A meeting can be arranged in either your own home or at your branch of the bank.

The discussion may take an hour or so of your time but it could save you a lot of worry and money in years to come.

Fill in the coupon overleaf and we'll send you more information.

SWAP YOUR SHARES FOR SOMETHING MORE INTERESTING.

Direct investment in the stock market can be risky, and keeping track of your own stocks and shares, complex and time-consuming.

So why not exchange your stocks and shares for units in a Barclays Unicorn Trust, of which there are 21 to choose from in the UK.

Not only will you spread your risks but you'll be relieved of much of the tiresome paperwork of certificates and tax returns.

Sound good? Indeed it is, but you'll never know how good unless you send the coupon overleaf.

With nearly 30 years' experience, and over £1,300 million managed on behalf of investors, we at Barclays are well qualified to advise you on your investment portfolio.

Simply complete this coupon, post it to us at the address below and we'll send you further details.

If you don't, you'll never know how much you stand to gain.

Please tick box:

☐ Please send me general information about Barclays Unicorn Unit Trusts.

☐ Please send me details of your Monthly Savings Plan.

☐ Please send me details of your Personal Equity Plan.

☐ I have more than £20,000 to invest and am interested in advice from one of your District Services Managers.

☐ Please send me details of your Share Exchange Plan.

To: David Chapman, Barclays Unicorn Limited, Juxon House, 94 St. Paul's Churchyard, London EC4M 8EH.

Name_____

Address_____

_____

_____ Postcode_____

Telephone_____

BARCLAYS

BARCLAYS UNICORN UNIT TRUSTS

Chapter Ten
Winning Strategies

So much choice, but how do you start picking out the winners from the also rans? There are several popular theories commonly aired. Here's a selection of the most frequently voiced strategies plus an assessment of their value.

Small is Beautiful

According to this school of thought, once a trust becomes large it is virtually impossible to make it outperform the market in which it is invested by a substantial amount. The reasoning is two-fold. First, you need lots of winners to make an impact on unit prices. Second, individual share holdings tend to be very large which limits the scope for dealing. Third, the portfolio becomes so diffuse it is more difficult to manage. Adjusting a common phrase slightly, the proof of the pudding is in the statistics. If you look at the top ten performing trusts in each of the five years between 1980 and 1985, twenty-four out of fifty slots were occupied by trusts with less than £5m under management.

Year	1981	1982	1983	1984	1985
Trust under £5m in the Top Ten	6*	5	3*	3	7*

*in each of the years 1981, 1983 and 1985 the size of one trust was not known but was assumed to be less than £5m.

Source: Barclays Unicorn

71

These figures are very much what you would expect to see if small trusts were performing no better and no worse than their larger cousins. Their representation in the league tables parallels the percentage of trusts with less than £5m across the industry as a whole.

As Good as New

For a range of reasons new trusts often outperform their competitors. The rationale is complex. First, new trusts tend to be small. Second, new trusts are often launched at a time when the fund managers think the investment fundamentals are right. Third, new trusts are often flagships for a group's marketing campaign.

The figures support the argument. Although only eighteen out of the top fifty slots between 1980 and 1985 have been occupied by trusts in their first complete calendar year of existence this is statistically higher than would be expected. The trend is towards more new trusts featuring in the big spots, with five out of the top ten trusts for 1985 being newcomers.

Year	1981	1982	1983	1984	1985
Newcomers in the Top Ten	2	3	4	4	5

Source: Barclays Unicorn

Winning Streaks

Fund managers tend to promote trusts which have just won a top place in the performing tables. But are these trusts likely to maintain their record? Here the statistics provide the clearest of all responses, no. Only two trusts between 1980 and 1985 are featured more than once in the top ten trusts over those years.

Last Year's Loser

In contrast to those managers who advertise a trust on the back of last year's high flying performance, there are some advisers who argue that history is perverse. They say you can find this year's winner hidden among last year's losers.

To check out the validity of this thesis, first look at the number of trusts which moved from either the top ten one year to the bottom ten the following year or made the switch in the other direction. Out of the ninety trusts which featured in the top ten slots over the period 1976–1984, ten had slumped to the bottom ten the following year. In contrast, only seven out of the ninety occupants of the ten bottom slots during these years rose to feature among the winners in the following year.

So much for the narrow interpretation of this theory. Taking a more broad brush approach, let's see what happens if we consider movements from the top ten one year to the bottom fifty the following year and vice a versa.

Apart from 1976 when all top ten trusts subsequently sunk to the bottom fifty the following year the evidence is not very convincing. Twenty-six out of ninety top trusts during 1976–1984 sunk to the bottom fifty without trace the following year. Far fewer – just nineteen – made the reverse trip ascending from the bottom ten to the top fifty the following year.

Award Winners
If you scour the papers for investments you can't help but come up against trusts proudly proclaiming to be the 'so-and-so' trust of the year or coming from an award winning group. The trouble is there are so many awards given by newspapers and magazines these days, that it's getting rather like showbiz, nearly everyone can claim their moment of glory and it's often pretty subjective.

Follow the Fund Manager
This is a tactic increasingly adopted by financial advisers. It's fine if you've picked the right country or speciality to invest in and provided the fund's performance did indeed reflect the expertise of an individual rather than a team. There is some evidence to suggest it is possible to pick a dozen or so fund managers who have consistently delivered the goods but often factors outside their control, such as whether there is a flow of new money into

MOVING UP

	1976	1977	1978	1979	1980	1981	1982	1983	1984
From Bottom 10 to Top 10 the following year	1	3	2	None	None	1	None	None	None
From Bottom 10 to Top 50 the following year	5	3	5	2	1	1	2	None	None

MOVING DOWN

	1976	1977	1978	1979	1980	1981	1982	1983	1984
From Top 10 to Bottom 10 the following year	3	None	4	None	2	None	1	None	None
From Top 10 to Bottom 50 the following year	10	None	7	None	3	4	1	1	None

the trust, can make it difficult to assess their individual contribution. Also, on international trusts most major groups now divide the function of stock selection from that of currency management, making it difficult to back the fund manager alone.

Bottom Line

The lessons to be learnt from this mass of theories and statistics tend to be rather negative. There is no easy formula for success. On the whole top performing funds which hit the very highest positions tend to sink almost into oblivion shortly afterwards. Small unit trusts can outperform large ones if they are invested in the right markets at the right time and if the fund managers decide to focus their attention upon these trusts. There is also growing evidence accumulating since 1983 that newcomers, especially from large groups with sophisticated marketing techniques and international investment muscle, can perform better than trusts which have been in existence for several years.

Lower Risk

Here's a few suggestions for those who prefer a more cautious path.

1. Go for a general UK trust.

2. Pick a trust which invests in established companies and is not heavily weighted towards any one sector or industry.

3. To avoid the problem of deciding when to invest choose a monthly savings plan linked to a general UK trust.

4. Stick to large well-regulated markets.

5. Avoid extra currency risks by staying in the UK.

Higher Risk

For those prepared to accept the higher risks involved in a spurt for growth, here are a few tips to keep in mind.

1. Shares tend to do better in the long term than fixed rate stocks such as government securities or bonds. So choose a trust

which invests solely in shares rather than one predominantly or partly in fixed rate stocks.

2. Smaller companies have greater profits growth potential than large to medium sized ones. Opt for a trust in your chosen market which emphasises smaller companies rather than a broad mix.

3. There are greater profits to be made from volatile markets than calm ones. Try to take advantage of sharp swings in sentiment to invest when prices are cheap and sell when they are high.

4. When trying to choose between two markets with equally sound economic and financial backgrounds, go for the smaller one. They tend to rise more sharply than larger, more developed and more locally driven markets.

5. Buck the herd instinct with care. Last year's loser is not necessarily this year's potential high flier. Go behind the figures to see what makes a market or sector really tick.

Chapter Eleven
Common Questions Answered

Short Term Choice

Q *I have some spare cash available for two months. Which type of unit trust should I invest it in?*

A None. Unit trusts are not suitable for short term investments. When you invest in a unit trust you pay charges and tax, which together reduce your capital by around 5%. That means just to come out even after two months the units would have to have risen in price by 5%. If you check back over past performance figures you'll see how rare this size of increase is over such a short period. Put your money in a high interest bank account or building society instant access account.

Investment Trusts v Unit Trusts

Q *Can you tell me the difference between a unit trust and an investment trust?*

A Yes, although it's easy to confuse the two, they are very different types of investment animals. First, let's look at investment trusts. These are companies run by directors and owned by share-holders. There are a fixed number of shares in issue. Their price depends upon supply and demand as well as moving in line with the rise or fall of the underlying share portfolio. Investment trusts make their money by buying and selling shares in other companies. Second, unit trusts. These are funds jointly run by unit trust managers and trustees. The unit trust manager takes the investment decisions, markets the trust and arranges for the sale of the units to the public. The number of units rather than the price in issue increases and decreases to reflect the demand. The trustee keeps a watchful eye on behalf of the unit holder to see that the managers stick to their brief and administer the funds fairly. The trust is owned by the unit holders and the units are priced in an agreed formula directly related to the value of the trust's share portfolio. Whereas investment trust shares may be priced above or below the value of its assets.

Chasing the Certificate

Q *I bought units in a trust four weeks ago and still do not have a certificate to prove it. What can I do?*

A If you have received your contract note, be patient. It's not much use writing to the fund managers as most delegate this process to someone called a registrar, often a bank or insurance company. Most groups take around six weeks to send out certificates but if there has been an extra demand – say at the time of a launch – they may be even slower.

The Right Price

Q *Why are there two prices quoted for most unit trusts and four for some others? Which is the right one?*

A Well, let's start with the most common situation of two prices. The higher or offer price will be the one you are charged when you wish to buy units. Included in this price will be the initial charge normally 5%. The lower or bid price is what you will be paid when you come to sell. Some groups complicate matters further by issuing two types of units and therefore having two sets of offer and bid prices. One lot of units, known as income units, will distribute their income to investors in the normal way and the other type, accumulation units, will add the income net of basic rate tax into the price. You will still receive a voucher showing how much tax has been paid on your behalf. It does not make any difference to the total return on your money which type of units you buy. It is simply a matter of convenience and whether you prefer to receive an income from your trust regularly.

78

American Disaster

Q *I invested in an American unit trust in 1985. Although the market did quite well my units did dreadfully. Why was this?*

A When you invest overseas, there are two ways you can make – or lose – money. First, on the shares themselves, and second, on the currency. Although many unit trust groups are extremely adept at picking shares, few have much proven expertise in currency. No one noticed this much in the early eighties when the pound was weakening as they just enjoyed windfall currency profits. Now the situation is less clear cut, currency management is becoming a critical factor in distinguishing the top performing managers from the mediocre.

Investors' Progress

Q *How can I check on the progress of my investment?*

A Most quality newspapers publish daily prices. You can also phone the managers for a price at any time. In addition you will receive two reports from the managers each year. The report will begin with an assessment by the managers of the trust's recent trading and a look into its future prospects.

Monthly Income

Q *Can I get a monthly income from a unit trust?*

A There are only a handful of trusts with this facility. As an alternative most groups offer a package of trusts aimed at producing income which together will give investors a payment each month, although not always of equal amounts.

Instant Access

Q *Can I withdraw my money straight away from a unit trust?*

A Yes. Unit trust managers can only invest in a range of shares and stocks which can be easily sold. So barring unforseen events, such as the closure of the stock market where the shares are traded, you can have access to your money straight away. Taking account of the paperwork you'll probably have to wait about a week for the cheque.

Kids In

Q *Can I buy unit trusts for a minor?*

A Yes. Put the units in the parent's name and use the child's initials as identification. You can buy units in a child's own name once they have reached 14 but this is not advisable as these units cannot then be sold until the child is 18. You can covenant either the income or the unit trust themselves to a minor, as long as he or she is not your child. This is an ideal route for grandparents or godparents. By using a covenant the sum invested will be boosted by 29%.

Risks Abroad

Q *Are international trusts more risky than UK trusts.*

A Yes, for the sterling investor. There are three risks. One, the shares will fall in value in local currency terms. Two, the shares will fall in terms of sterling. Three, the exchange itself may suffer problems which rebound on share prices. For example, at the end of 1985 the small and undeveloped Singapore and Malaysia exchanges ran into liquidity problems and share prices took a tumble.

Extra Income

Q *I have money with a building society and am trying to increase my income. I noticed that several gilt trusts pay a higher yield. Should I switch?*

A The first point to remember is that when you put money in a building society you earn interest. Then when you want to withdraw your savings you are repaid exactly the same as you deposited. With a unit trust, even one invested in gilts, you cannot be sure how much your units will be worth when you come to cash them in. For example, if gilt prices fell as interest rates rose you could find that although you earned a higher yield, you lost some of your capital. Also remember, that gilt trust yields are quoted gross, before tax, whereas building society interest is paid and quoted net of standard rate tax.

Portfolio Size

Q *Can you tell me when I buy units in a UK trust how many companies I will have a stake in?*

A There is no exact figure. The number of holdings can be as low as 20 or over 100. One rule which puts a floor on the number of holdings is the regulation that states no share stake must acount for more than 5% of the fund's portfolio at the time of purchase.

Safety Standards

Q *How safe is my money when I invest in a unit trust?*

A Unit trusts are one of the most secure ways of obtaining professional management of a share portfolio. All the trust's assets, that's shares and cash, are held in the trustee's name and it is the trustee who issues certificates on the fund. Of course, there are no guarantees about how good the fund managers will be, the losses can occur through poor invest- ment decision or overall market movements.

Dial-A-Price

Q *I have just bought some trusts. I ordered them over the phone direct from the unit trust manager on a Monday. When I checked the price at which I had bought them it was different from the one quoted in Monday's papers. Why was this?*

A The prices for each unit trust are calculated daily on the basis of the value of the fund's shareholdings as verified by a stock- broker. The price you saw in Monday's paper was therefore Friday's dealing price.

Performing Miracles

Q *Looking through the newspapers I have seen two different trusts both claiming to be the top performing UK trust. How can they both make such claims?*

A When looking at advertisements for the unit trusts which include comparisons there are two key factors. One, on what basis is the rise in unit price calculated. The standard is now the difference between the offer, or purchase price and bid or sale price. Some groups, however, still base their figures on offer to offer, which usually boosts the results by about 6%. Two, look at the period involved. Unit trust prices fluctuate daily and over a single year may gyrate from month to month.

New Gloss

Q *Most unit trust advertisements are for new funds. Does this mean the manager thinks now is the best time to invest in this particular fund or are they merely advertising it because it's new?*

A Most trusts have an incubation period of about six months. So new trust launches can reflect the manager's views of nearly a year ago. Also, markets can change quickly. New trusts sometimes take a while to invest unit holders money so some groups may advertise in anticipation of conditions becoming more favourable. If in doubt, ask the manager whether they intend to become fully invested quickly.

Cashing In

Q *I bought units in an international trust two years ago. I was very surprised to read an article that the trust manager had sold 35% of its shares and put that money on deposit. If I had wanted to place my money in a building society I would not have gone to the trouble and expense of buying uinits. Are they allowed to do this?*

A There is a debate raging within the industry about just how much of a trust's money managers should move out of shares if they think the market is about to fall. It is very rare indeed for an international trust to be so heavily uninvested. Ask the fund managers what their policy is on this matter.

Charge It

Q *I have had shares in a particular trust for five years. I've just received notice of an increase in charges from ½% to 1%. That's a 100% pay rise for the managers. Why don't I have a say in this?*

A When the trust was set up a ceiling for its charges was included in the trust deed. Whenever investors were invited to put money in the trust they had to be told the current charges and the maximum permitted under the trust deed. Managers can raise their fees in line with those specified in the trust deed by giving unit holders three months notice. High increases require unit holders consent.

All Change

Q *The trust which I invested in was taken over by another group. I now hold units in a different fund. Does the switch count as a sale for tax purposes.*

A No. As far as the taxman is concerned there has been no sale. You should take a close look at the quality of the new company and make sure you are still happy with your investment.

Taxing Issue

Q *Some groups advertise a tax-free income scheme. Is this a good idea for someone who is retired and needs a growing income?*

A Right, let's look first at how this so-called tax free income scheme works. It is based on the idea of selling off a certain number of units twice a year and paying out the proceeds as an income. Provided you have not exceeded your capital gains tax allowance then this 'income' will be tax free. What is happening is that you are being paid part of your capital as income. Assuming the scheme allows you a 15% income, unless the price of the units rises by more than 15% you will have eaten into your capital. What's more if prices fall, you could lose all of your capital. A better bet is to divide your money between a deposit account with a higher initial income than you can obtain on shares and an income fund which should pay out a growing income over the years. Some groups now market packages just like this.

Monthly Options

Q *I started an insurance linked monthly savings plan about twelve years ago and found when I tried to stop after a few years that I could not get my money out. Will this happen if I open a unit trust monthly plan?*

A You can stop, start or skip payment with a unit trust monthly plan. There are a few points to watch out for. Check the charges The majority of groups simply deduct the standard 5% fee but some subtract up to 20%. Most groups reserve the right to cash in your units and repay you the funds if the amount saved is less than a stated minimum.

Starting Point

Q *How much money do you need before you can invest in unit trusts?*

A The minimum investment varies from group to group. There are two ways of going about it. You can agree to save a fixed sum each month which can be anything from £20 upward or you can invest a lump sum of £500 or more. Most groups quote an exact sum as the minimum they will accept but a handful of groups still insist you buy a minimum number of units, so you will need to check the price to work out the smallest permitted investment.

Income Tax

Q *Do I have to pay tax on any income I receive from my unit trust investment?*

A The income will be paid after standard rate tax has been subtracted. If you do not pay tax UK residents can reclaim the money paid out on your behalf. Higher rate taxpayers will have an additional tax bill.

Capital Gains Tax

Q *Will I have to pay tax when I sell my units and when I switch between unit trusts in the same group?*

A Any gains you make on the sale of units are subject to capital gains tax. When you switch between unit trusts of the same group this counts as a sale and new purchase. Provided your capital gains for the year do not exceed your allowance there will be no bill. For the large active investor one way to limit your tax liability is to use what is called an offshore umbrella fund which consists of a range of sub-funds without throwing up a tax bill. Alternatively, if you are happy to leave the switching decisions to the fund managers you can opt for a general UK trust or so-called managed fund which consists of a portfolio of trusts run as a single unit trust group.

Chapter Twelve
Reading Between the Lines

You can keep track of the price of your units by checking in most quality newspapers over the weekend or ringing the managers direct. Do remember that there will be two prices quoted for each unit, the higher or offer price at which managers are prepared to sell units to the public and the lower or bid price, which is what managers are prepared to give you if you wish to sell. Some unit trusts offer two classes of units, income and accumulation. If you buy income units you will receive distributions, normally twice a year. However, if you opt for accumulation units then your income will be allowed to accumulate net of standard rate tax. So accumulation units are always standing at a higher price than income units. In investment terms there is no difference in overall return, it is simply a matter of personal choice.

Price Check

When checking the price, keep a note of the original price you paid. It is on the contract note. Then you can compare this with the price it would cost you to buy the units today and the price you would receive if you decided to sell your units. All the buying and selling costs are rolled up into the quoted price, so you do not need to add on any extra charges before working out the value of your holding.

Apart from the two sets of prices, you will also find the yield quoted. This is based on the flow of dividends in the previous year worked out as a percentage of the current offer price. It should be used as a broad indication of what you can expect to receive by way of income. Obviously the quoted yield will fluctuate in line with changes in the value of the units and the patterns of dividends payments made by the companies in which the trust was invested. The yield you receive will depend on how much you paid for the units in the first instance.

Report and Accounts

For most unit holders the key to enlightenment comes through the letter box once a year in the form of the trust's report and accounts. At first glance this can seem rather offputting. A mass of statistics and dreary economic commentary. Don't give up, its worth perservering. The report will tell you:

- how the trust is performing in absolute terms and by comparison to some (hopefully) suitable share or bond index
- what the managers think about its future prospects
- what holdings they have, which they have sold and maybe where they intend to invest in the coming months.
- how fully invested the trust is at present and whether some of your money is sitting uninvested on deposit with a bank
- if it is an overseas trust, you'll find out about its currency exposure
- practical information about the yield, distribution dates
- names and addresses of the manager, trustee, registrar, auditor
- full details of the portfolio, broken down into appropriate sectors.

So much for the text, you'll also find two pages of figures. One headed capital account and the other income and distribution statement.

a. *capital account.*
From this you'll be able to tell whether the trust was growing or shrinking. How much new money was coming into the fund, how many holdings were sold and whether profits were boosted by other sources such as underwriting commission.

b. *income and distribution statement*
this monitors the flow of income in and out of the trust. On the plus side will be income from dividends and interest on

deposits, on the minus side is the managers annual charge and VAT on this. Then there will be deductions for tax paid on dividends and income. This net amount will be used as the basis for calculating the sums due to unit holders in the form of distributions.

HOW PERFORMANCES VARY

Returns on £1,000 Investment Over One year to January 1st 1986*

	Best	Worst	Average
UK General	+29%	− 9%	+13%
UK Growth	+61%	−10%	+13%
UK Equity Income	+35%	+ 1%	+15%
UK Mixed Income	+22%	− 2%	+13%
Gilt and Fixed Interest Growth	+ 9%	− 1%	+5%
Gilt and Fixed Interest Income	+10%	− 4%	+ 3%
Investment Trust	+12%	+ 5%	+10%
Financial and Property	+38%	+ 4%	+18%
International	+51%	−13%	+ 5%
International Income	+13%	+11%	+ 2%
North American Growth	+28%	−32%	+ 2%

Europe Growth	+71%	+ 5%	+44%
Australian Growth	− 9%	−28%	−21%
Japan Growth	+30%	−17%	+ 6%
Far Eastern Growth	+27%	−43%	− 5%
Commodity and Energy	−10%	−33%	−19%

* Net income reinvested

Source: Money Management (rounded to nearest full decimal point)

Matching the Index

You will get a good idea of how your units are faring by keeping a regular check on the price and reading the manager's report and accounts. A good fund manager should be able over the long term to outperform the average return in any given market or sector.

When comparing a trust's performance against a chosen index, there are several points to keep in mind. First, the cost of dealing is included in the price of a trust but not in an index. Second, unit trust prices are usually boosted by assuming that income has been reinvested. Third, the make-up of an index may distort comparisons with a trust. For example, the FT Ordinary Index consists of thirty leading companies. It would be wrong to compare it with the price pattern of say a UK smaller companies trust.

Figurework

However, since the unit trust industry has become increasingly cut-throat managers tend to try and outwit their competitors. The aim is to be the top performing unit trust group overall and capture one of the valued prizes dished out by the newspapers to the winning unit trust group each year. There are usually as many different winners as there are prizes as it depends on how the figures are worked out and which starting dates are chosen.

In the past most groups used to quote their performance figures in terms of the increase in offer price of the units over a given period. This indicated the rise in the underlying share portfolio of the trust. More recently the industry has switched to quoting the difference between the original offer price and the final bid price, which reflects the actual return to investors over the period assuming they sold their units at the end of the time allotted. The result of this change was to reduce overall performance by around 5½% on average and to show up the importance of holding units for a reasonable period of time in order to benefit from the underlying growth in the trust's portfolio.

Making comparisons

Several magazines and newspapers produce tables of best performing trusts, sometimes without attempting to classify these into sectors. Don't let these figures mislead you either into a fit of unfettered optimism or a cloud of depression. Every year, for reasons varying from luck to judgement, a handful of trusts turn in outstanding performances.

They achieve returns way above what could be expected from a trust investing in a broad range of shares in a given market. If the trust in which you have invested does not come up to this standard don't despair. First, see how it compares to the market it has chosen to invest in and then if you are not satisfied, compare its performances to other trusts in the same sector with the same objectives. A good trust will consistently feature among the top third of its particular sector. Those considering investing should not be lured by the expectation of being able to match last year's top performing trust. Go back and check the performance of the average fund. This will give you a much sounder foundation upon which to plan your investment strategy.

Chapter Thirteen
On the Tax Free Track

The idea that everyone should have a stake in British industry has been one of the mottos of the Thatcher government. To try and encourage more people to invest directly in shares the chancellor, Nigel Lawson, unveiled in his 1986 budget preliminary details of a new tax free scheme, called Personal Equity Plan. The scheme is designed to overcome many of the obstacles ordinary shareholders face such as the voluminous paperwork, the need to fill a detailed tax return and the mathematical contortions required to assess any capital gains tax bill. Instead, the administrative burden and need to keep the Inland Revenue informed has been transferred onto the broad shoulders of the companies such as banks, stockbrokers and unit trust managers who will be operating the scheme.

At the moment it is up to every individual to report any transactions which may throw up a tax bill to the Inland Revenue. For unit trust investors the two points to watch are whether there is an extra bill to be paid on any distributions they receive and whether the capital gains they realise in a particular year exceeds their individual allowance.

Authorised unit trusts pay their distributions net of basic rate tax, which means along with your payment you will receive a credit that proves the tax bill has been settled. Higher rate taxpayers will have an additional sum to pay, while non-taxpayers will normally be able to reclaim the tax paid out on their behalf. Any gains made by selling your units for a higher price than you bought them count towards your total capital gains. The tax year does not start on January 1 but April 6th. For each tax year every single person or couple can make a specified sum of capital gains tax free. Additional gains are then taxed at 30% after deducting any increases which merely match inflation.

So, for example, let's say you invested £50,000 in a top performing unit trust, such as Barclays Unicorn General Trust on March 1, 1982 and sold your entire holding on March 1, 1986. The capital gains tax allowance for the tax year 1985–6, which this sale falls into, is £5,900. You work out your gain by deducting the cost of the original units, ie £50,000 from the price you received when you sold £133,880 and then adjust this figure to take account of inflation over the period of your investment, and of the equalisation payment arising on the first income distribution. You will then pay capital gains tax on £67,458 ie £73,358 – £5,900 which at 30% gives a bill of £20,237.

PEP Talk

The Inland Revenue and Treasury have put their heads together to devise a set of rules which will apply to Personal Equity Plans once these are introduced on January 1, 1987. Initially the government intended the plans to be vehicles for channelling money into British companies quoted on the London stock market, but it bowed to pressure and agreed to include authorised unit trusts and investment trusts, subject to specified ceilings.

●*Who can invest?*
You must be over eighteen and normally resident for tax purposes in the UK. Certain people who are temporarily non-resident because they are working overseas for the government, perhaps as diplomats, will be able to participate. Even though husbands and wives share a single capital gains tax allowance, each of them will be able to start a plan.

●*How much can you invest*
You are only permitted to invest in one plan each calendar year and the maximum sum that can be placed on the plan is £2,400 in cash. It is not possible to save up your annual allowance and add it to the following year's total. Nor are you allowed to split your money between several different plans in any single year. You can, if you wish, transfer your plan from one accredited manager

to another, but you should check to see if any charges are billed for this service.

● *What investments can be held in the plan?*
According to the governments guidelines you can invest all your money in shares quoted on the London stock market. Alternatively you can channel a small proportion, £35 a month or 25% of your total investment, into authorised unit trusts and investment trusts. Through authorised unit trusts you will be able to invest in a wide range of shares and fixed interest securities, including companies quoted in New York, Tokyo, Hong Kong, Sydney, Malaysia, Singapore and Continental Europe.

● *What are the benefits?*
Any capital gains on your investment and all income from your shares or unit trusts will be rolled up within the plan tax-free, provided the money remains invested for the full period specified. The qualification rules are slightly confusing. You must keep your money in the plan over a full calendar year. This means if you invest in March 1987 you will forfeit your tax free status if you withdraw cash from the plan before December 31, 1988. You are free to swop holdings within the plan at any time you wish, as long as this does not upset the balance between shares, unit trusts, investment trusts and cash. One slight curiosity is that any money which has been invested in shares cannot at a later date be switched into unit trusts or investment trusts, even if you have not exceeded the stated limits which apply to these two vehicles.

Interest earned on univested cash will also be rolled up tax free provided you stick to certain ground rules. When you first put money into the plan it has to be in the form of cash. If your investment is £2,399 or less you can leave this sum uninvested earning tax free interest in a specially designated account. This will pay interest gross and will be a segregated account, from which the plan managers can only withdraw cash if they wish to invest on your behalf. After you have paid £2,400 into your personal equity plan the cash must be invested within twenty-eight days and in any event by December 31 of the year in which you started the plan.

Slightly confusingly the rules change once you start investing. From then on you cannot keep more than a specified amount in cash within the plan for more than twenty-eight days. The cash ceiling is the greater of either £240 or 10% of the plan's value at the end of the previous calendar year after making any deductions for cash withdrawals, once these are allowed. For example, on December 31, 1989 your three-year-old plan is valued at £4,800. You can then keep up to £480 in cash during 1990 without losing out on the tax benefits. Let's say in June 1990 you withdraw £1,200 to pay for your holiday. Your cash limit will then be reduced to £360. If you were to withdraw£3,000 then your cash ceiling would be fixed at £240 for the rest of the year.

●*What information will you receive?*
At least once a year you will be sent a full statement of your investments, the price at which they were bought and their current value, plus details of any cash held in your plan. Every time a share or unit is bought for you the plan managers will send you a contract note with the price and all the details. You will also receive the annual reports from any companies or unit trusts in which your money is invested.

●*How safe are the plans?*
Companies wishing to run personal equity plans have to overcome two hurdles. First they must be authorised to deal in securities. This means passing muster either with the newly formed Securities and Investment Board, the City's self regulatory body, or one of the so-called SROs, self regulating organisations which have been set up to cover specific industries. Second, they need to have obtained a registration certificate from the Inland Revenue, which is to ensure the administrative formalities are met.

In addition the plan manager will have to conform to strict rules about the handling of customers money and investments. They cannot for example pool your cash with theirs and leave it sitting in a bank account to be withdrawn for the manager's own purposes. It must be clearly separated and identified in a special customers' account. Although investments in shares can be grouped together and held in the plan's manager nominee name, you must be cleary indentified as the ultimate owner of the shares or unit trust.

Finally, there are strict regulations about the price you can be charged for your investments. According to the Inland Revenue rules they must be purchased at open market prices. This means the best available price at the time in the case of shares and the quoted offer price which includes the initial charge for unit trusts. You will be able to check these prices by looking at your contract note and comparing this with the prices quoted in the papers for the particular unit trust or the price given in the Stock Exchange's Daily Gazette for shares.

●*How to choose a plan*
Two types of plan will be on offer, although some groups may not choose to market both sorts. First, and probably most common, will be what are called discretionary plans. This means you will leave the investment decisions to the plan managers. Discretionary plans will probably be tailored to meet certain clearly defined needs such as income, growth or overall return. Second, there will be plans which allow you to make your own investment decisions. Some of these may restrict you to choosing just unit trusts, while others will give you full range to manage your money. Plans which give you scope to take a free hand may be few and far between because fund managers argue the costs involved may well outweigh the benefits. With strict rules on how long uninvested cash can remain on deposit the fund managers say costs would quickly mount if they had to badger DIY enthusiasts to reinvest within a certain time span.

If you are going to choose a discretionary trust there are two main criteria; the plan manager's investment capability and the charges. Traditionally it has been very difficult to assess the performance of portfolios run by brokers and intermediaries as the information is not freely available and each case tends to be different. However, a rough guide can be found by looking at a group's record on management of other funds such as unit trusts or pensions. On charges it will be much more clear cut. Most plans will probably have an upfront charge which is deducted from your initial investment before it is placed in the personal equity plan and then an annual charge subtracted from income generated within the fund at the end of each calendar year. You should also check with care the interest rate you will earn on your cash. Under the rules this must be paid gross but there is nothing to say that it should be in line with the rates you could earn on say a high interest account.

On plans where you make your own decisions the charging structure is likely to be rather different. In theory the initial charge should be smaller or non-existent and you should pay a fee per transaction and an annual sum to cover administration based on the value of your investment.

Another point to watch is whether there are charges if you wish to transfer your plan to another registered manager. You can do this at any time without forfeiting your tax relief or generating a sale for tax purposes. Overall, you should do a few sums to weigh up the tax benefits of the plan against the charges. Let's look at a few sums. Assuming you are not a large investor you will probably be unlikely to pay capital gains tax, so your tax savings come from dividends and any interest on uninvested cash. Assuming the gross yield on shares is 5% and you invest the full £2,400 in shares, your tax saving will be £34.80 in the current tax year (1986/87). You will also save on broker's fees which could amount to a further £35. Now against this you must balance all the charges on the plan. If the initial charge on he plan is 3% ie £72, and the annual fee is ½% – equal to £12 assuming your money had not grown – your savings will have evaporated. Unit trusts already include both annual fee and an initial charge in the unit price. Here you should be comparing simply the tax saving ie £8.70 on a maximum permitted investment of £600 with any plan costs. This means avoiding unit trust personal equity plans with additional charge of 2% or more.

For higher rate taxpayers personal equity plans are better value, especially if they opt for high yielding shares and unit trusts. People who are enjoying the age allowance will find there will be advantages in being able to convert income and interest, which could have reduced their additional allowance of untaxed earnings, into a tax-free gain.

Where to Get PEPs

Although a large number of institutions will in theory be permitted to offer personal equity plans, it is unclear at the moment how many will actually grab the chance. There is a hefty administrative burden involved and only those with specifically tailored computer programmes are likely to be able to meet the Inland Revenue's requests for information. The most likely contenders are banks, the top ten biggest building societies and independent unit trust groups.

Barclays Bank, for instance, will be marketing a Barclayshare Personal Equity Plan from January 1, 1987. This will be a discretionary service available for people who wish to invest either just in unit trusts or solely in shares. The unit trust version will be for people with between £20 and £35 a month. There will probably be no additional charges over and above those included in the unit trust itself. Your money will be invested straight away. The share version will be for monthly savers with between £40 and £200 or lump sum investors with between £420 and £2,400. Here your money will be managed. It may be left on deposit in the specially designated personal equity plan account until the managers think it is right to invest, subject of course to the rules governing the plan being met. You can choose whether to have your money placed in a single quality share or divided between four and five if you are investing a lump sum. For monthly plan holders their money will be invested in between three and six shares. You will be able to specify whether you wish your holdings to be chosen with growth, income or overall return in mind. However, remember you cannot withdraw any money by way of dividends or cash, so everybody is effectively looking for the maximum overall return regardless of how it is made. Those who prefer lower risks are therefore probably best off going for the income option.

What can you gain

For the unit trust investor it seems a pity not to take advantage of these new tax free plans, particularly if there is no additional initial charge or a very small one of say under 1%. To compare the return on a unit trust investment within a personal equity plan to one outside, take a look at an investor who placed £35 a month into the Barclays Unicorn General Trust on June 1, 1981 and left it there for five years, their units would have risen to be worth £4,469.50 which includes reinvested income net of basic rate tax. If personal equity plans had been invented in 1981 and the same money channelled through one of these plans, assuming no extra charges, the total value of their holding would be £4,611.25. So you would have increased your return by £141.75.

Glossary

A

Accumulation Units

There are two types of units available in most unit trusts. These are accumulation and income units. Accumulation units are designed for investors who do not wish to receive dividend cheques. Instead the dividends minus basic rate tax are accumulated into the price of the units. That's why if you look at tables of unit trust prices you will often find two different prices for units in a single trust. The accumulation units will stand at a higher price than the income units. Holders of income units receive a stream of dividends, usually twice a year.

Agent

The agent is an intermediary or third party, such as a licensed dealer or member of the Financial Intermediaries, Managers, Brokers Regulatory and Investment Managers, who sell the products of several companies. A large proportion of unit trust sales in this country are completed by agents, who in turn are paid commission for their trouble by the groups whose merchandise they sell.

Authorised Unit Trust

Before a unit trust can be marketed to the public in this country it must be vetted by the Department of Trade and Industry to ensure that the company running the trust is suitable and the trust itself conforms to current rules. Only once a trust has the Department of Trade and Industry's seal of good housekeeping can advertisements for it be placed in the newspapers.

B

Back to Back Loans

A tool used by unit trusts with overseas portfolios who think that the currency in which they have invested is about to weaken against sterling. In order to prevent what it considers to be currency speculation the Department of Trade and Industry will only allow unit trust managers to use back to back loans as a method of protecting foreign shares against adverse currency movements. As the name suggests two transactions are involved. First, the group deposits sterling with a bank and then it arranges to borrow the equivalent amount in foreign currency. This allows the fund managers to lock in their commitments at a specific exchange rate.

Bid Basis

One of the key features of a unit trust is that the price of the units reflects the value of the fund's shareholdings. When a trust is shrinking managers will calculate the price of units on what is called a bid basis. This means the price for each holding will be the amount the managers could expect to receive if they sold those shares. Managers are reluctant to price their trusts on a bid basis as it lowers the value of units and can adversely hit the trust's performance record.

Bid Price

The price at which you can sell back your units to the managers. It is lower than what is called the offer price – which is the amount you would have to pay if you wish to purchase units.

Book

The name given to the stock of units held by unit trust managers. Unit trust managers are responsible for both creating and cancelling units. They do not have to cancel units when these are sold. If the managers prefer they can simply buy back the units and hold on to them until the demand picks up. Unit trust managers only tend to hold units in trusts where they expect the price to rise.

C

Capital Gains Tax

Individuals who make a profit from selling a capital asset such as shares, unit trusts or a second home must pay tax on any gains over and above the standard allowance. Unit trusts do not have to pay capital gains tax on profits made from buying and selling shares.

Certificate

About four to six weeks after the purchase of units in a trust you will receive a certificate. This is proof of ownership. It will show the number of units you hold in a specified trust and will be signed by the trustee.

Charges

Under the current rules unit trust managers must clearly state all the charges involved. There is normally an initial charge of between 5% and 5¼% which is deducted from the money you invest plus an annual charge of between ¾% and 1½% which is subtracted from the trust's income.

Commission

Unit trust managers reward intermediaries who sell their trusts with payments called commission. The standard rate of commission on lump sum investments is 1¼% and in addition licensed dealers and members of Nasdim receive 1¾% marketing allowance for fully qualified advisers. Most groups pay the same rate on monthly savings plans. The commission is paid out of the initial charge on the trust. As the unit trust industry is growing more competitive some groups are starting to pay commission above 3%.

Concentration

A unit trust's portfolio is said to be concentrated if holdings are kept down to a minimum. One of the requirements of unit trust managers is that they spread investors money between a range of shares in order to minimise the risk. They are not allowed to divert more than 5% of the fund's money into a single company.

Contract Note
This should arrive within days of any purchase or sale of units. However, investors in regular monthly savings plans receive a six monthly statement showing units purchased in the period. It will show the number of units bought and the price plus the total sum due. Don't lose the contract note as you may need it later on to show the taxman.

Cum Distribution
Units are bought cum distribution in most cases. As old Latin hands may remember cum means 'with'. When you buy units cum distribution you are automatically entitled to any future distributions of income. All units are sold cum distribution unless the letters 'xd' are printed by the price.

Current Yield
The distributions due in one year expressed as a percentage of the price of the units. The yield is usually quoted gross, that's before any tax has been deducted. That does not necessarily mean it will be paid gross. Distributions on unit trusts are paid net of standard rate tax but unit holders who do not pay tax can reclaim the sum paid on their behalf. Most offshore funds pay their distributions gross but this is still subject to tax at your standard income rate.

D

Dealings
The term used to describe the purchase and sale of units in a trust or fund. Most unit trusts can be dealt in daily but if you are planning to buy an offshore fund do remember to check the dealings days. Many of these funds can only be dealt in once a week.

Dictum Meum Pactum

My word is my bond. The operating motto of the Stock Exchange where huge transactions are concluded by word of mouth. A large percentage of unit trusts deals are also concluded on this basis.

Discount

When a unit trust company launches a new trust or embarks on a sales drive to promote a particular fund it may offer the units at a discount. This means investors pay less for the units than normal. Discounts are financed out of the initial charge deducted from unit holders money. So if the initial charge on a trust was 5% and the group offered a 1% discount, investors are effectively paying a lower initial charge of 4%. The discount is usually given in the form of extra units. The term bonus is used interchangeable with discounts.

Distributions

Payment made to unitholders out of the trust's income. Distributions are paid net of standard rate tax but non-taxpayers can reclaim the tax paid on their behalf.

Distribution dates

The dates when dividends are distributed to unit holders. This is usually six weeks after the amount of the dividends has been announced. Most trusts pay dividends twice a year but a handful of income trusts pay quarterly. There are even a couple of income trusts which pay dividends monthly.

E

Equalisation

Equalisation applies only to units purchased during a distribution period. It is the average amount of income earned by a unit trust and included in the price of all units purchased between distributions. When holders of those units receive their first distribution of income this sum is refunded as a return of capital. Being capital it is not liable to income tax but must be deducted from the cost of the units for capital gains tax purposes.

Ex Distribution

In the period just before distributions are paid out to unit holders the units in the trust are usually bought and sold ex-distribution. That means that new buyers are not entitled to receive the distributions. Before buying units you should check both the distribution dates and the day the units go ex-distribution. Investors looking for growth are usually best advised to buy units ex-distribution as the price will fall slightly once the money has been paid out.

Exempt

Certain trusts and funds are exempt. Units in these can only, be sold to non-taxpayers, such as charities and pension funds, as they enjoy special tax privileges.

Expropriation

The term used when units are cancelled. When a unit trust holder sells a holding the fund managers have the choice to buying the units for themselves or cancelling the units. If the units are cancelled then part of the fund is expropriated.

Extraordinary General Meeting

A meeting of unit holders must be called if vital decisions affecting their investments are to be made. 21 days notice must be given in advance. Extraordinary general meetings are necessary before charges can be increased above the maximum level laid down in the Trust Deed, or the trust's investment criterion changed radically.

F

FIMBRA

The Financial Intermediaries, Managers, Brokers, Regulatory Association. This is a self-regulatory body which consists of a wide range of companies. Membership can be checked at its headquarters at 22 Great Tower Street, London EC3R 5AQ. At present there is no compensation fund in place for its members.

Fixed Offer Price

This is normally associated with the launching of a new trust, although you may occasionally come across the term during a special promotion of a particular trust. When a unit trust company decides to launch a new fund it normally sets aside about three weeks to raise the first batch of money. During this period, it will sell units at a fixed price. In the past, groups have sometimes advertised units in an existing trust at a fixed price but they usually reserve the right to alter this offer if the price of the units changes dramatically

Franked Income

When a trust receives dividends from its shareholdings in UK companies, these have already been subject to corporation tax. In order to avoid such dividends being taxed twice, they are referred to as franked income and no further corporation tax liability is incurred.

Futures

Contract to buy or sell a certain commodity at a fixed price at a specified date in the future. Authorised unit trusts are forbidden to invest in futures but offshore funds are usually free to do so.

G

General Trust

The label given to unit trusts which either invest in a broad range of UK companies or a wide spectrum of international markets. These contrast with so-called specialist funds, which channel money into specific types of companies eg high technology or leisure, or which focus on a single market eg Germany or Australia.

Gilt Trust

Special tax concessions are available to trusts designed to invest solely in UK government securities, known as gilts. The income earned on gilts is taxed at basic rate level within the fund rather than being subject to the higher corporation tax rate.

Growth Trusts

These are trusts which pay a very low income and concentrate on increasing the price of the units. Most overseas trusts are usually growth orientated, although just recently a number of groups have introduced international trusts specially for investors seeking a combination of income and growth.

H

Hedging

The term used to describe action taken by a fund manager to protect a trust's holdings against adverse currency movements. Unit trust managers are restricted in the way they can hedge funds to the method of back to back loans. Offshore fund managers can choose between various methods including futures, options and back to back loans.

Holdings

Another term for share stake. For example, if a trusts largest investment was in ICI, you could say it's biggest holding was in ICI.

I

Income

The money unit holders receive by way of distributions is called income. It is taxable at their current level of income tax. Unit trusts with above average yields are referred to as income or high income funds.

Income Units

These are units in a unit trust which distribute their dividends to investors. They are contrasted with accumulation units where the income is rolled up into the price.

Income Trusts

These are trusts where the main aim is to produce a high and growing source of income for investors. Many groups have put together packages of income trusts so that holders can enjoy a monthly income.

Initial Yield

When a trust is launched the managers will estimate the amount of income they will pay in the first year. This is done by calculating the income they would have received if they had held their chosen stocks over the past year after deducting sums to cover their annual charges.

Investment Trust

A company which invests in other companies. The price of shares in an investment trust quoted on the stock exchange will depend upon the supply and demand for its shares as well as moving in line with the rise or fall of the underlying share portfolio. Unlike unit trusts, investment trusts can borrow money and have greater freedom to invest in a wide range of securities, option, futures and commodities. They can be purchased through a stockbroker and the charges are the same as on standard share transactions.

L

Licensed Dealer in Securities

At the moment in order to sell securities – that's shares and unit trust – companies must either be stockbrokers, banks, members of the trade assoctiation FIMBRA, Financial Intermediaries, Managers, Brokers Regulatory Association, or licensed by the Department of Trade and Industry as bona fide dealers. Under the government's current proposals on investor protection the department will delegate its responsibilities in this area to self regulatory bodies composed of financial institutions. In the meantime, if you wish to check whether a company does hold a license then a list is available from HMSO, PO Box 276, London SW8. Price £6.30

Listed Company

A company whose shares are listed on a recognised stock exchange. Unit Trusts have to follow strict rules on the type of shares in which they can invest. These are designed to limit the risks and make sure that a unit trust manager will always be able to sell his holdings and repay investors if asked.

Liquidity

The amount of cash available for investment. In most trusts this is usually around 5% but a new trust may have larger amounts of liquidity as it can take several weeks to become fully invested. If the market in which a trust specialises appears to be about to drop the managers may increase liquidity. However under the current rules the Department of Trade and Industry frowns upon any unit trust which goes liquid to the extent of more than around 30% for a prolonged period of time.

M

Management Charges

There are two charges on most trusts. First, an initial charge which is included in the offer price of units sold to new investors. Second, an annual charge deducted from the trusts income. This is based on a percentage of the trusts size. Practices vary across the industry, some groups calculate the fee monthly but deduct half yearly while others assume the trusts will be growing continually and therefore calculate it half yearly and deduct it twice a year. New unit trust groups who need the extra cash flow may deduct the fee monthly. Full details can be found in the trust deed and should be stated in promotional literature and the managers report. The deed will also specify a ceiling above which the fund managers cannot charge. Many trusts are launched with a certain annual charge but include a provision for an increase up to a stated amount in the trust deed. When the trust is marketed the managers must tell the public what the maximum permitted charges are. Three months notice must be given to unit holders of increases in charges up to the level agreed in the trust deed.

Managers

The unit trust management group is responsible for launching, marketing and managing the money in its stable of unit trusts. It must also make a daily market in the units pricing them according to a formula laid down by the Department of Trade and Industry.

Minimum

Unit trust groups are free to set a minimum sum for each trust. Most groups now require investors to place between £500 or £1,000 in each trust. For smaller investors there is the less onerous starting point of between £20 and £50 involved in a monthly savings plan.

O

Offer Basis

This is the standard method of calculating the value of a trust. It assumes a fund is growing and prices the underlying value of the shares at the sum it would cost to buy them.

Offer to Bid

When considering the return on a unit trust investment this is the crucial set of figures to look at. First, you take the cost of the units – that's their offer price and then subtract this sum from the disposal proceeds, that's their bid price. The difference will be the actual profit a unit holder will have made. Most groups in the industry now use figures calculated in this way when advertising the past performance record of their trusts. If you are trying to compare the returns on various trusts do make sure the figures you are assessing were calculated in this way.

Offer to Offer

This is a way of measuring the overall performance of the trust rather than the return to investors. Some groups still use this method of calculation when advertising their trust's performance, especially when comparing their performance to an index which obviously does not reflect dealing charges. This can be rather misleading as it ignores the charges incurred by investors and will boost the return by around 5½%.

Offer Price

The price at which units are sold to the public. It includes any initial charge on the trust.

Offshore Fund

A fund operated outside the jurisdiction of the UK authorities. Offshore funds, in contrast to the more strictly regulated unit trusts, cannot be marketed freely in this country. They usually pay dividends gross, their charges vary considerably and the quality of the fund managers is not uniform.

R

Registrar

Many unit trust groups employ outside registrars to carry out some of the paperwork involved in running a unit trust. This includes issuing the trust certificate and sending out distributions. The larger groups may carry out these tasks in-house.

Regular Savings Plans

Most groups run monthly savings plans for investors with sums above £20 a month who want to build up a lump sum. The schemes are very simple and flexible. You simply decide in advance how much you wish to save every month and set up a standing order. There is usually no penalty for missed payments and you can have access to your money straight away. Some groups reserve the right to cash in your units and repay you if you stop making monthly contributions while you still have only a small sum of say less than £400 in your plan. Most groups make no additional charges for monthly savers but it does pay to double check the fees first.

Reinvestment

Some groups offer investors the choice between income units, where distributions are paid out, and units where the distributions minus basic rate tax are used to buy additional units.

Rounding Charge

An adjustment in the price of units in a trust to avoid unwieldy fractions. Managers of authorised unit trusts must limit this rounding up to 1.25p or 1%, which ever is less. Offshore funds may have greater discretion. Check the small print.

S

Sector

Unit trusts are classified in various sectors to enable fair comparisons to be drawn between the performance achieved by an individual trust and its direct competitors. The criteria range from requiring a particular geographic spread to insisting on a yield either higher or lower than the stock market as a whole.

Share Exchange Scheme

Under these schemes shareholders in major quoted companies can swop their individual stakes for units in a trust. It is important to remember that such a switch is treated as a sale as far as the taxman is concerned and could throw up a capital gains tax bill. Most unit trust groups will only accept a limited range of shares under these schemes and before choosing this route compare the price you will get for your shares from the unit trust group with a standard sale through a stockbroker.

Spread

The difference between the offer price at which units are sold and the bid price at which units are bought back from the public is known as the spread. It reflects the initial charge plus any stamp duty or sales tax. On most UK unit trusts the spread is around 6%

Subdivision of Units

Unit trusts are normally priced in pence. When the price of a particular trust has risen to the equivalent of several pounds many fund managers think it is more convenient to split the units into smaller denominations. This does not alter the value of your holding or the overall size of the trust.

Subscription Day

Most unit trusts are dealt in daily which means you can buy and sell units on any day of the week. However, many offshore funds limit transactions to a single day, known as the subscription day.

Switching Discount

A discount given to investors switching betwen different trusts run by an single management group. Normally when money is switched the investor ends up buying units in the new trust at the offer price which includes the standard initial charge. To encourage loyalty and reduce the element of double charging most groups halve the initial charge when you switch funds.

T

Tax Credit

When you receive distributions from a unit trust you will also be sent a tax credit to show that 29% tax has been paid on your behalf. If you do not pay income tax, you can reclaim the amount paid. Remember to keep the tax credit in a safe place as evidence for the taxman.

Traded Options

An option that is quoted in the traded options market run by the Stock Exchange. Unit trusts are allowed to use traded options to a limited extent. Many offshore funds have greater freedom to use options as they please. The traded options market is very risky and unit trust managers are restricted so that unit holders are not exposed to unexpectedly high risks.

Trust

A group of people or institution which looks after the investments of another. Under the law of trusts there are strict regulations governing their behaviour and the way they carry out their obligations.

Trust Deed

This is the legal document between trustees and the fund manager which lays down the framework within which the managers must operate. It specifies the investment restrictions and charges.

Trustees

Institutions such as banks or insurance companies of proven integrity. Their role is to ensure that the managers keep to the rules laid down in the trust deed and where necessary to defend unit holders' interests. Their fees are paid by the managers out of the management charges. In the case of authorised unit trusts, the trustee must be independent of the fund management company.

U

USM

Unlisted Securities Market. This is the junior version of the stock market designed for companies who wish to have their shares available to the public in a regulated way but do not qualify for a full listing. In particular it enables relatively young companies where the owners do not wish to lose control of the business to tap public money.

Umbrella Fund

The name given to an offshore fund which offers a range of shares in various sub-funds under a single umbrella. The advantage for investors is that you can switch between sub-funds without throwing up a capital gains tax liability.

Unauthorised Unit Trust

A fund which has not been authorised by the Department of Trade and Industry. It cannot be advertised or marketed in the UK.

Underlying Holdings

These are the shares held by the unit trust on behalf of investors. The price of the units is calculated by direct relation to the market value of these underlying holdings.

Unfranked Income

Income which in the hands of a UK unit trust becomes subject to corporation tax. Trusts which only invest in gilts, local authority and fixed interest stock are required to pay basic rate income tax rather than the higher rate of corporation tax.

Unit Allocation

When you buy an insurance policy which is linked to a fund not all your money is invested in units. The unit allocation will determine how much of your money is placed in the fund and how much goes to cover the insurance element and marketing expenses.

Unit Trust

A fund authorised by the Department of Trade and Industry. Its main aim is to invest in equities and there are strict rules governing its other investment activities. The trust is owned by unit holders and the price of their units are directly related in an agreed formula to the value of the trust's shares. The number of units is increased or decreased to reflect the flow of money in and out of the fund. The units are priced in such a way that the value of each unit in relation to the fund is unchanged. Unit trusts can be freely marketed in the UK and they do not pay capital gains tax on their internal share dealing.

Unit Trust Association

It is partly a self-regulatory body set up by the unit trust industry. It lobbies on the industry's behalf to government and runs an information service for customer. Unit Trust Association members manage 96% of the money in unit trusts.

Unit Trust Instrument Duty

A rather archaic tax, ¼% of new money added to the trust. It is payable by the managers to the taxman and is included in the difference between the buying cost of units.

Unitisation

The conversion of an investment trust into a unit trust. The costs of such an operation is usually equivalent to about 6% of the investment trust's assets so it is only worth doing if the price of the shares in the investment trust are substantially lower than the net assets per share.

W

Withdrawal Scheme

A system under which regular payments can be obtained from a unit trust investment. This is achieved by the sale of units. This may be more tax efficient than going for a high income unit trust but it can result in a decline in the real value of your capital very quickly if the trust's overall performance lags the rise in retail prices.

Y

Yield

The yield on a trust is calculated on the basis of the anticipated flow of dividends and interest from its existing holdings. First, the total income from shares is added up and then the managers fee is deducted. This sum is then expressed as a percentage of the current offer price giving a gross prospective yield.

USEFUL ADDRESSES

THE ADVERTISING STANDARDS AUTHORITY LTD
Brook House
2–16 Torrington Place
London WC1
Telephone: 01-580 5555

ASSOCIATION OF CORPORATE TRUSTEES
L. C. Howes Esq. Secretary
2 Withdean Rise
Brighton
Sussex
BN1 6YN
Telephone: Brighton (0273) 504276

DEPARTMENT OF TRADE AND INDUSTRY
1–19 Victoria Street
London SW1
Telephone: 01-215 7877

FIMBRA
22 Great Tower St
London
EC3R 5AQ
Telephone: 01-283 4814

THE STOCK EXCHANGE
Old Broad Street
London
EC2N 1HP
Telephone: 01-588 2355

UNIT TRUST ASSOCIATION
Park House
16 Finsbury Circus
London EC2M 7JP
Telephone: 01-638 3071
Association of Corporate Trustees

COUNTRYWIDE ADVICE AVAILABLE

For information on Barclays Unicorn Unit Trusts contact your local Barclays Unicorn District Office, listed below:

Birmingham District:
63 Colmore Row
Birmingham   B3 2AA
Tel: (021) 236 4000

Bristol District:
3rd Floor 14/16 Queen Square
Bristol   BS1 4NT
Tel: (0272) 297799

Exeter and Truro Districts:
6 Bedford Street
Exeter   EX1 1LN
Tel: (0392) 52288 Extn 437

Leeds District:
1st Floor
Barclays House
6 East Parade
Leeds   LS1 1HA
Tel: (0532) 445641/2

Liverpool District:
PO Box No 26
2nd Floor
4 Water Street
Liverpool   L69 2EX
Tel: (051) 236 2151

London (South):
Eagle House
1/2 Parkshot
Richmond
Surrey   TW9 2RN
Tel: 01-940 0131

London (North):
Crown House
47 Chase Side
London   N14 5BE
Tel: 01-882 6321

Luton and Chelmsford Districts:
PO Box No 4
Crystal House
Crawley Road
Luton   LU1 1HL
Tel: (0582) 424122 Extn 3351

Maidstone and Brighton Districts:
22 Mount Sion
Tunbridge Wells
Kent   TN1 1UE
Tel: (0892) 47877

Manchester District:
2nd Floor
50 Fountain Street
Manchester   M2 2AP
Tel: (061) 832 6717 Extn 195

Newcastle and Darlington Districts:
4th Floor
Bamburgh House
Market Street
Newcastle-upon-Tyne   NE1 6BH
Tel: (0632) 328614

Norwich and Ipswich Districts:
Lawrence House
St Andrew's Hill
Norwich   NR2 1HQ
Tel: (0603) 660255 Extn 5571/5573

Nottingham District:
Chapel Bar House
1/5 Maid Marian Way
Nottingham   NG1 6AL
Tel: (0602) 415121

Oxford and Reading Districts:
North Bailey House
4th Floor
New Inn Hall Street
Oxford   OX1 2RS
Tel: (0865) 246207

Peterborough and Cambridge Districts:
29 Market Place
Market Deeping
Peterborough   PE6 8EA
Tel: (0778) 345465/6

Preston District:
Unicentre
Lords Walk
Preston   PR1 1DH
Tel: (0772) 52199

Shrewsbury District:
Crown House
St Mary's Place
Shrewsbury
Salop   SY1 1DU
Tel: (0743) 53901

Southampton District
Office 16
12 Bargate Offices
Southampton   SO1 0DN
Tel: (0703) 223505

South Wales District
PO Box No 65
Golate House
101 St Mary Street
Cardiff   CF1 1BU
Tel: (0222) 378151

Aberdeen District:
1 Rubislaw Terrace
Aberdeen   AB1 1XE
Tel: (0224) 648347

Glasgow District:
1st Floor
90 St Vincent Street
Glasgow   G2 5UQ
Tel: (041) 221 8691/2

For information on investment services (£50,000 and above), personal taxation, wills and trusts contact your local Barclays Bank Trust Company Office, listed below:

PO Box No 34
63 Colmore Row
Birmingham   B3 2BY
Tel: (021) 236 4000

Lees House
21/33 Dyke Road
Brighton   BN1 3FE
Tel: (0273) 778911

14/16 Queen Square
Bristol   BS1 4NS
Tel: (0272) 277711

2 Regent Street
Cambridge   CB2 1DA
Tel: (0223) 315315

PO Box No 2
Golate House
101 St Mary Street
Cardiff   CF1 1RG
Tel: (0222) 378271

Aquila House
Waterloo Lane
Chelmsford
Essex   CM1 1YB
Tel: (0245) 353244

Ninth Floor, Grosvenor House
125 High Street
Croydon   CR9 1RP
Tel: 01-686 4477

Barclays Bank Chambers
63/67 Terminus Road
Eastbourne
East Sussex   BN21 3NG
Tel: (0323) 641222

6 Bedford Street
Exeter   EX1 1LN
Tel: (0392) 52288

171 High Street
Guildford
Surrey   GU1 3AN
Tel: (0483) 505656

PO Box No 1
Eagle House
19 North Street
Havant
Hants   PO9 1QJ
Tel: (0705) 473741

2nd Floor
Lowgate House
Lowgate
Hull   HU1 1JJ
Tel: (0482) 224035

Crown House
Crown Street
Ipswich   IP1 3HR
Tel: (0473) 211277

PO Box No 14
9 Highgate
Kendal
Cumbria   LA9 4HA
Tel: (0539) 23805

Central Trust Office
Radbroke Hall
Knutsford
Cheshire   WA16 9EU
Tel: (0565) 3888

Barclays House
PO Box No 1
6 East Parade
Leeds   LS1 1HA
Tel: (0532) 440951

PO Box No 149
6 Water Street
Liverpool   L69 2HB
Tel: (051) 236 5428

'Ferndale'
2 Trinity Square
Llandudno
Gwynedd   LL30 2PY
Tel: (0492) 74477

Kinnaird House
1 Pall Mall East
London   SW1Y 5AX
Tel: 01-930 2383

Crown House
47 Chase Side
Southgate
London   N14 5BE
Tel: 01-886 5468
      01-882 5254

PO Box No 4
Crystal House
Crawley Road
Luton   LU1 1HL
Tel: (0582) 424122

Brenchley House
123/135 Week Street
Maidstone
Kent   ME14 1PQ
Tel: (0622) 54351

PO Box No 306
50 Fountain Street
Manchester   M60 2BT
Tel: (061) 832 6717

3rd Floor
Bamburgh House
Market Street
Newcastle-Upon-Tyne   NE1 6BH
Tel: (0632) 617676

Lawrences House
St Andrews Hill
Norwich   NR2 1HQ
Tel: (0603) 660255

Chapel Bar House
1/5 Maid Marian Way
Nottingham   NG1 6AL
Tel: (0602) 411481

North Bailey House
New Inn Hall Street
Oxford   OX1 2RS
Tel: (0865) 724611

29 Market Place
Market Deeping
Peterborough   PE6 8EA
Tel: (0778) 347982

Parkville House
Red Lion Parade
Bridge Street
Pinner
Middx.   HA5 3JX
Tel: 01-868 1322

Old Orchard House
39/61 High Street
Poole
Dorset   BH15 1BG
Tel: (0202) 671167

5 Market Way
Reading   RG1 2BN
Tel: (0734) 55844

PO Box No 30
Eagle House
1/2 Parkshot
Richmond
Surrey   TW9 2RN
Tel: 01-940 8421

Crown House
St Mary's Place
Shrewsbury   SY1 1DU
Tel: (0743) 53901

29/31 Kingston Road
Staines
Middx.   TW18 4LH
Tel: (0784) 56524

27/29 Greenhill Street
Stratford-Upon-Avon
Warwickshire   CV37 6LE
Tel: (0789) 204371

12 Walter Road
Swansea   SA1 5NP
Tel: (0792) 466203

3 Pydar Street
Truro
Cornwall   TR1 2AR
Tel: (0872) 72209
      (0872) 73091

Crown House
15 The Broadway
Woodford Green
Essex   IG8 0HL
Tel: 01-505 4645